# *A* Father-Saving SON

## THE STORY OF A PRODIGAL OF A PRODIGAL

**Tony R. Murfin**
*With Zackery Murfin*

WESTBOW
PRESS®
A DIVISION OF THOMAS NELSON
& ZONDERVAN

WestBow Press books may be ordered through booksellers or by contacting:

WestBow Press
A Division of Thomas Nelson & Zondervan
1663 Liberty Drive
Bloomington, IN 47403
www.westbowpress.com
1 (866) 928-1240

ISBN: 978-1-5127-9665-0 (sc)
ISBN: 978-1-5127-9666-7 (hc)
ISBN: 978-1-5127-9667-4 (e)

Library of Congress Control Number: 2017911109

Print information available on the last page.

WestBow Press rev. date: 11/9/2017

## Dedication

I dedicate this book first and foremost to my only begotten son,
Zackery Murfin, a beautiful work of God. Zack and I dedicate
this book to the prodigal sons and daughters of prodigal sons
and daughters of generations past, present and future…

# Contents

# Preface

*A Father-Saving Son* came into being through the faithfulness of God and the obedience of a son.

I had just returned from Tulsa, Oklahoma, on my first journey out to see my son Zackery at Dick's Correctional Center. It was through the divine guidance of the Holy Spirit and two-way journaling that I received confirmation through a word of knowledge from above. "All Zack has ever needed is the love of his Father. Go feed my sheep!"

I vividly remember that as I got up off the dock to go write my son a letter, I clearly heard the Voice of Truth tell me: "I said, 'Go feed my sheep!'" Zack didn't need another lifeless letter and more words from his father; he needed only the love of his Heavenly Father. It was quite clear that God was guiding me to go visit my son and feed him with spiritual food through God's word.

God spoke and I listened. I gave my son the words of his Father and explained to Zack that he wasn't doing his time backward; he was living his life backward. I gave him every word spoken to me, and we both stood amazed at the life that these divine truths brought to us both. There were many confirmations along my travels that confirmed that God was moving.

Upon returning home I was scheduled to serve as a Prayer Cha on a Tampa Bay Area Emmaus Walk men's retreat. I was responsible for the prayer room, for preparing communion elements and praying in/out each speaker who gave a talk on God's grace. These talks were given by both laity and clergy; five talks a day throughout the three-day weekend.

I was ready to pray in our first clergy speaker, who was to give the talk on "Prevenient Grace." It was John V., a local pastor and brother in Christ. We were in a holding pattern, waiting for the talk room to notify us that they were ready for John. We sat in the chapel, shooting the breeze, when the Holy Spirit impressed upon my heart to share my recent trip to Tulsa and all the Jesus encounters along the way.

As I began to invite this retired veteran and F-16 fighter pilot into my adventure of going out to see my son in prison, he stood in amazement and spoke these words to me as his eyes filled with tears: "Please tell me you have written this all down somewhere! Tony, promise me you will have this testimony printed and made into a spiritual tract or booklet that can be used in prison ministry as an encouragement for other men and women who sit without hope for the future in our country's correctional institutions."

The Monday after the Emmaus Walk weekend, I was awakened at 2 a.m. by the living utterance and unmistakable voice of God. "Tony, get up and write." Needless to say, I got up and began to write down this small story as a tract or booklet. As I began writing I asked God the name that John spoke out in chapel that day, "A Father-Saving Son." It certainly would fit the story I was being led to tell. So, I added the subtitle, "The story of a prodigal of a prodigal."

But God gave me a bigger vision than a booklet, and the story flowed out of me like rivers of living water. So, there it is: the *how* and the *why* of this book. I hope and pray that it blesses you and the multitudes …

# Acknowledgments

To the Almighty Father; His Son, our Savior Jesus Christ and the Holy Spirit: Thank you for abundant life and for creating us anew as Your always-being-loved sanctified sons. It has only been through Your living, breathing voice that has continued to lead, guide, mold, shape, refine, teach, comfort and empower us, that this life work and story could ever have been scribed. We pray it may bear everlasting fruit for Your banquet table and Your ultimate praise, glory, and honor.

To the one daughter He breathed out and knitted together so divinely, the one He set apart to make me the whole Tony I am today, my lover and my life-companion, my best friend and the most amazing mother on planet earth, my loving wife, the Beautiful Bimini: Thank you for the fervent prayers you prayed that led me to my knees, and the arms of Christ; for always standing by me and encouraging me to reach higher for His best for our marriage, for our children, family, and the ministries He has entrusted to us. Most of all thank you for making the forgiveness of Christ and His everlasting grace real in my life.

To the incredible men who have invested in me spiritually and who have poured themselves into my life and mentored me from a prodigal man to a surrendered son: I am truly blessed, as there is not enough space in this book to list you by name; but each of you knows who he is: someone used by the hand and voice of God to make me a disciple and discipler of others.

To St. Skipper "Captain Woodrow Call" Hair for your tenacious love and endless pursuit to get me to write and express in words all that Abba Papa desires to pour out through me upon the world He so loves: Thank you, precious brother, for always being there to lift my arms when they have grown weak, to pray alongside me when my feeble knees gave way, and to see in me what I couldn't see in myself. You inspire me to be all God created me to be in Christ. You are His navigator to the world around you, always guiding lost souls to freedom in Christ Jesus.

To two of the most incredible shepherds on this planet: Dr. Joey Mimbs and Pastor Dave Geisler, who took the time to equip me and multitudes of others with God's truth, which the Spirit used to build a foundation in Christ that can and will never be shaken or taken from me: Thank you for endless hours of patience, understanding and enduring through all my "whys and how comes." Thanks to your precious wives and children who shared you and allowed you to give yourselves away so freely to me and the flocks with which you've been entrusted. You have surely made knowing my Lord and Savior Jesus Christ so simple and easy, even a child like me could understand.

To the countless spiritual leaders around the world who have been formed and planted all around me by the Lord like oaks of righteousness, also my C-12 brothers, my River Wilderness brothers, my Friday Morning Men's group in the Upper Room, my Emmaus brothers and sisters, and a host of pastors, teachers, and evangelists around the world: Thank you all for allowing me to see the Love of Christ in/through each of you!

To the God-given and gifted editors that helped me pull this book together and make it the best it could be—thank you Jacqueline Spierenburg, Patricia Hill and Doc Hensley.

# Foreword

Our Heavenly Father makes things beautiful and amazing. By His description, Tony Murfin's first 46 years were anything and everything but. But God (and this book is full of divine intervention) saw who Tony now is, in Christ. And His New Life in Tony is all of beautiful and amazing.

*A Father-Saving Son*, the story of a prodigal of a prodigal, is a story within a story within a story. The Greatest Story of why and how the Son of God came to seek and save His lost children surrounds Tony's account of deliverance from the prison of "a pleasure-seeking paradox," a prodigal lifestyle with no boundary or satisfaction. Flowing from Tony's story is that of his son, Zack, a convicted felon, sought and saved by that same Son. By the amazing provision of God the Father, His Son saved a father and his son through a beautiful Poured-Out Life.

*A Father-Saving Son*, the story of a prodigal of a prodigal, chronicles Tony's heart change and the ways God made Himself real in Tony's life. Then God pours His love through Tony into Zack, in a prison cell. Tony's journaling and correspondence reveal Zack's change from inmate to in-Christ.

I asked Tony if he had ever noticed what his name spells backward. Yes, he has. He was quick to reply, "Y-not!" I am so glad God saw Tony, of whom many would have scoffed, "No way," and said, "Why not?"; that He saw Zack and said, "Why not?"; that He saw me, also, and said, "Why not?"

We need A Father-Saving Son.

"And He will turn the hearts of fathers to their children, and the hearts of children to their fathers, lest I come and strike the land with a decree of utter destruction." Malachi 4:6 ESV

Patricia Kae Hill
Apollo Beach, Florida, August 30, 2016

# Foreword

*Inside these walls* ... lies a heart of a boy but inside the boy is the heart of Jesus Christ waiting to love him.

*A Father-Saving Son* is a story that reveals how God is never too far from reaching out His love, even if you are in the darkest, most dangerous place as far as you can be from Him. When you call on God's Son, Jesus Christ, His love will transform you.

As God sent His only begotten Son to be a sacrifice for the world's sins, Tony had struggled to let go of his son, only to have him return one day in the most amazing way. Zackery's letters from inside the walls of prison reveal the amazing transformation that can only take place when a father sets out to save his son.

Tony once experienced the same dark struggles that Zack did, as Jesus did in coming to this Earth; but together through the heart of Almighty God and only by His grace, mercy, and love for these three men has transformation occurred.

As you read this story, *A Father-Saving Son*, allow the Holy Spirit to move you "to enter the playfulness into which we are all being wooed and summoned." Almighty God will "bring us to places our hearts and minds cannot begin to fathom or conceive." We are "clearly created for something more, supernaturally more!" Tony and Zack are definitely on the path of something supernaturally more.

Inside this story, you will feel the heartfelt love of a father for his son and the love of the son for the father, united together with the love that only comes through Jesus Christ.

Zackery walked into prison as a boy with no hope and a heart barely murmuring. He learned how to live "Inside Out" to become a man on fire for Jesus Christ.

As you read this story of the father and his son, you will be invited to take part in their transformation from darkness to the Light of Christ burning strong and bright.

I trust you will be entertained, moved and inspired, as I was, by the faith, hope, and love of "*A Father-Saving Son.*"

Sharing in the love,

Gayle Zinda

# CHAPTER 1

## In the Beginning

The word *prodigal* means, spending money or resources freely and recklessly; wastefully extravagant; having or giving something on a lavish scale. I was that prodigal, as I wasted God's provision and His inheritance. I didn't realize I was rebelling against Him. But God is a gracious, heavenly Father. His lavish provision for me included the extravagant generosity of His Son, Jesus.

My first forty-six years were simply the generational epidemic of a prodigal father walking in the footsteps of his prodigal father, who is now raising his prodigal son.

Hundreds and thousands of years of this generational perversion called independence is from the same deception (and Deceiver) that led to humanity's falling in the garden long ago. It's nothing new under the sun. It's the very godlessness of a compromising world living in separation, perversion, and the brokenness where we find ourselves wading today. Yes, it is the fallacy of the *self-life*, and a lie that we can be our own gods!

Let's face the facts—every naturally created being to walk the face of the planet came into the world as a son or daughter separated from God through the lineage of Adam and the forbidden Tree of the Knowledge of Good and Evil. We are the seed that chooses against God's best for what appears to be greener pastures. So our "in the beginning" story is merely how we belong to a much greater story: the story that existed before "in the beginning."

Humanity didn't come onto the scene until the second chapter of *History*. Before "in the beginning" and the creation of the universe, the Father, Son, and Holy Spirit enjoyed an eternal relationship, characterized by His essence: love and glory. Before creation, the heavenly host (angels) and the kingdom above were formed. Before our "in the beginning," a third of them followed the leadership of the greatest of them, Lucifer (a.k.a. Satan), who rebelled against heaven and the Almighty Father of light, His Son, King Jesus, and the living, breathing voice of the Holy Spirit. Before creation as we know it, the Triune God knew that humankind would join this rebellious movement of the fallen angels and would be ruined to the point of death by the fall, becoming unholy, evil, corrupt, and spiritually bankrupt. It would become separated from it's Creator.

But God had a redemptive plan for all humanity before "in the beginning!" The plan involved the begotten Son of God's incarnation, His perfect life, and His perfect sacrificial death. His plan was life in the form of a gift of grace to be received or rejected by choice through faith so the world He so loves could be restored. A remnant of human beings would/will choose to be united with their King and become the holy and blameless sons and daughters of God, spiritually fit companions for the eternal glorious God.

So what is our response to God's glorious purpose in creating us, redeeming us, enriching us, and glorifying us for all eternity? It is to be holy, set apart, and sanctified vessels who live to reflect our callings and divine purposes as sons and daughters of the Almighty God, created in His very image before the foundation of the world. Our response leads us to praise, adore, and honor our Master with worship and surrendered hearts. And we go out into all the world and echo the light, love, and life of Christ to all creation.

Author Erich Sauer wrote,

> "These mighty words stand in the Scripture not
> for the satisfaction of curious inquisitiveness, nor
> even for the intellectual completion of our picture of

history of the world's salvation, but in order to show us the greatest of the divine love. Even before the ages of time, the Highest concerned Himself with your glory and with mine. Before the sea raged and swelled, before the earth was built or its foundations were sunk, yea, before those morning stars exulted and those sons of God shouted for joy, God, the Almighty, even then had thoughts on me. On me, the worm of the earth, who have given Him so much trouble and labor with all my sins; on me, He Who is God, the Ancient of days. Truly these are depths not to be fathomed, and which the heart of every man despairs of being able to describe in words. Here we can only bow and worship, and lay our life at the feet of Him, the All-Loving." [1]

The story I share with you is one of faith, hope, and love. It's a story lived out by many but proclaimed by few. It is the story of a multitude of rebellious fathers rearing rebel sons and daughters who live out of darkness in a deteriorating world that is perishing and spiraling out of control. It's a story about the realities of what the Father has done for the world He so loves. It's a story of both truth and freedom bestowed upon all creation simply to choose from what is black or white, a truth or a lie, the self life or the Christ life. The free choice either to receive or reject the greatest gift ever given is the gift of life and light itself.

This eternal life is found only in the Son, who was given through the loving grace of the Father and Creator of all things seen and unseen. His is the hand of the Bridegroom. It is given in eternal matrimony to have and to be held, from this day everlasting, through the mountains and in the valleys, for richer and poorer, in sickness

---

[1] Sauer, Erich. *The Dawn of the World Redemption: A Survey of the History of Salvation in the Old Testament.* London, England: Paternoster Press, 1951, 26.

and health. It is to love and to cherish as we grow into oneness, even unto death on a cross. Oh, to receive the mystery hidden for ages but now revealed for all creation to partake of His divine nature, the hope of glory—Christ in you!

# CHAPTER 2

## The Testimony of a Prodigal Father

"But in your hearts set apart Christ as Lord. Always be
prepared to give an answer to everyone who asks you to
give the reason for the hope that you have. But do this
with gentleness and respect, keeping a clear conscience,
so that those who speak maliciously against your good
behavior in Christ may be ashamed of their slander."
—1 Peter 3:15–16 (NIV)

For the better part of forty-six years, like the demon-possessed man
Jesus healed in Mark 5:19, I allowed Satan to control and rule my
life. I experienced every lustful and perverted pleasure this fallen and
dark world had to offer. I was a self-made, self-indulgent, prideful, and
arrogant entrepreneur. I was a shell of a man who didn't even have God
on the radar screen, yet I had been blessed from head to toe. I was as
lost and as far away from God as anyone could possibly imagine, never
realizing that Jesus was right there all along, just waiting and protecting.

"But God demonstrates his own love for us in this:
While we were still sinners, Christ died for us."
— Romans 5:8 (NIV)

Yet in the midst of the cocaine parties, the booze cruises, and the
hedonistic getaways in far and away lands, the Lord always had some

sort of hedge of protection around me. I tell you the truth: it's only by the grace of God that I am here today to witness to any of His works.

"Say to them, 'As surely as I live, declares the Sovereign LORD, I take no pleasure in the death of the wicked, but rather that they turn from their ways and live. Turn! Turn from your evil ways! Why will you die, O house of Israel?'"
—Ezekiel 33:11 (NIV)

"Here is a trustworthy saying that deserves full acceptance: Christ Jesus came into the world to save sinners—of whom I am the worst. But for that very reason I was shown mercy so that in me, the worst of sinners, Christ Jesus might display his unlimited patience as an example for those who would believe on him and receive eternal life."
—1 Timothy 1:15–16 (NIV)

I was possesed and in complete bondage to a thirty-six-year daily drug addiction, serious alcoholic bingeing, and living completely over the edge in what seemed to be an endless pleasure paradox and quest for happiness and fullness of life. I had been blessed by God with a wife who was a saint compared to me. I was also given a son and two beautiful little daughters, never realizing that the footsteps of children are sure to follow the footsteps of the father they know and love.

"For the creation was subjected to frustration, not by its own choice, but by the will of the one who subjected it, in hope that the creation itself will be liberated from its bondage to decay and brought into the glorious freedom of the children of God."
—Romans 8:20–21 (NIV)

I was consumed and controlled by the almighty dollar, of which there was no shortage in my life due to Ground Zero Electrostatics, a twelve-year-old global reach business that God groomed me into by 2008. It was my personal resource center for all the capital required to live the so-called "successful lifestyle," to which I was in bondage.

> "But godliness with contentment is great gain."
> —1 Timothy 6:6 (NIV)

Consumed to consume, the desire to acquire was my life. My resource center allowed me to live in fancy waterfront houses, to drive flashy cars, to drip with gold and diamonds, and to eat and play at the finest restaurants and country clubs. It allowed me to afford world travel and frequent Las Vegas getaways disguised as a businessman's busyness.

> "Do not love the world or anything in the world. If anyone
> loves the world, the love of the Father is not in him. For
> everything in the world—the cravings of sinful man, the
> lust of his eyes and the boasting of what he has and does—
> comes not from the Father but from the world."
> —1 John 2:15–16 (NIV)

By all the standards and values taught and accepted by the fallen world in which we live, I had reached the pinnacle of life and was living the so-called american dream. I worked hard and I played harder. Then God opened my eyes. My world was barren. It was a dead-end road that reeked of death and darkness. This was the night of my spiritual heart attack.

> "Praise be to the God and Father of our Lord Jesus Christ, the
> Father of compassion and the God of all comfort, who comforts
> us in all our troubles, so that we can comfort those in any trouble
> with the comfort we ourselves have received from God."
> —2 Corinthians 1:3-4 (NIV)

I sat in my living room that night, overshadowed by something I can't fully explain. It can be described only as a feeling and sense that my life here was over and that I was getting ready to depart from this place. It was euphoric and dreamlike. I wasn't dizzy but was completely conscious of my surroundings. It felt as if something was melting slowly over my entire head, as if a gallon of honey was being poured over me. A numbing sensation moved down my face, down my neck into my shoulders, down my chest and into the depths of my gut. In that second, I realized what it was. I was dying! Terrified, I screamed for my wife. I huddled on the floor with my wife Bimini and our little girls, Karagan and Kiah. In that moment I realized I truly loved these dear ones more than life itself. I cried out to Jesus not to take my life but I also asked Him to take care of my family because I knew I wasn't going to make it.

But my wife's faithfulness in dragging me to church for the past ten years was about to pay off. For ten years I had heard the Word of God proclaimed and nothing, not one single verse of Scripture, had ever stuck. It always fell upon deaf ears and a hardened heart. But in that moment, I realized that one thing did stick, the only thing I ever needed to know – His name, the name of Jesus Christ, Son and Savior. I remembered the Name above all names and called out for Him and He answered me.

"To the LORD I cry aloud, and he answered me from his holy hill." "The righteous cry out, and the LORD hears them; he delivers them from all their troubles." " ...and call on me in the day of trouble; I will deliver you, and you will honor me."
—Psalm 3:4; 34:17; 50:15 (NIV)

"Trust in the LORD with all your heart and lean not on your own understanding; in all your ways acknowledge him, and he will make your paths straight."
—Proverbs 3:5-6 (NIV)

"Salvation is found in no one else, for there is no other name
under heaven given to men by which we must be saved."
—Acts 4:12 (NIV)

God allowed me to reach the hospital where I underwent an
emergency heart catherization, multiple MRI's, and several brain
scans. I sat in that hospital for three days with nothing but time to
consider my life and how I had gotten to such a dark and desperate
place. In all my pondering I was awakened to the truth that I had
experienced all the world had to offer a man. I had acquired all the
shiny stuff in life, and I had experienced both fame and fortune. By
the worlds tape measure I was a successful entrepreneur, a self-made
man. But deep inside I knew I was the most miserable man on the
planet, void of peace and anything resembling lasting happiness.

Although there was never any medical explanation of what
happened on March 13, 2008, God opened my eyes to reality. He gave
me hope, stopped my madness, and delivered me from everything that
separated me from Himself. The only way to describe what happened
in that hospital over those three days is that God flipped some sort of
"off switch" inside of me and gave me a spiritual heart transplant. No
surgical procedure ever took place. I vividly remember calling out to
Jesus once again that Saturday afternoon. I figured He got me to the
hospital. What did I have to lose?

I said, "God, if You're really real … If you are here and you can
hear me right now… Make yourself real to me. Make yourself real in
my life!" It wasn't fifteen minutes later when the doctors walked into
my room and said, "Mr. Murfin, we don't know how to explain what
happened to you on Thursday night. All your vitals indicated we were
losing you, but after all the testing we've concluded that there's nothing
wrong with you. You're free to go." That's crazy, I thought to myself.

"I will give them an undivided heart and put a new
spirit in them; I will remove from them their heart of

9

stone and give them a heart of flesh. Then they will
follow my decrees and be careful to keep my laws."
—Ezekiel 11:19-20 (NIV)

"Therefore, if anyone is in Christ, he is a new
creation; the old has gone, the new has come!"
—2 Corinthians 5:17 (NKJV)

"I have been crucified with Christ and I no longer live, but
Christ lives in me. The life I live in the body, I live by faith in
the Son of God, who loved me and gave himself for me."
—Galatians 2:20 (NIV)

From there, God laid out a series of events that I can explain
only as supernatural and the divine plan of Jesus Christ for my life.
God had a cure for every disease in my life. Addictions as well as
broken and shattered relationships — with my wife, kids, mom, dad,
brothers and everyone I chose to use as pawns on a game board. He
also rid my business of the poison I had bred into it and endless other
things that I can't begin to list. Here are a few of His miracles in a
chronological order as He began His divine housecleaning in my life:

## His Off Switch

I was a three-pack-a-day smoker, a chronic pot user, a full-time cocaine
abuser and a binge drinker. In over thirty years of drug addictions,
I had experimented with all kinds of narcotics and hallucinogenics.
After March 13, 2008 and my three days in that hospital, I never had
the slightest desire to do any of these things again. God had set me
free and had broken the chains of bondage that had held me captive
all my life. He did all of this for His greater purpose and glory.

"I can do everything through him who gives me strength."
—Philippians 4:13 (NIV)

## His Housecleaning

Several days after getting out of the hospital, I was sitting at work and the Holy Spirit called me home to clean up. I went home and cleansed my house of all the world's temptations. I flushed the contents of my so-called "fun box" and poured out an entire private stock, gallons upon gallons, of Satan's assorted pleasures, poisons and toxins. Everything had to go, the cocaine, the crack, the skunk weed, the pills, the pipes and paraphernalia all got trashed with no remnant left behind.

> "But as for me and my household, we will serve the LORD."
> —Joshua 24:15b (NIV)

## Success that Mattered to God

My wife had signed me up for a men's conference titled, "Man in the Mirror — Success that Matters," months prior to March 13, 2008. I had no intention of ever going and actually had orchestrated an exit strategy for her Christian outing long before. However, the Holy Spirit planted me at the conference that Saturday morning. As I listened to one of the speakers give an account of his own out-of-control life, I thought to myself, "Surely there can't be two of us that have lived this kind of life?" There was an invitation to pray the prayer of salvation (a prayer I had prayed many times before). I made a second decision for Christ that weekend and I prayed a very similar prayer to the one I cried out back in March, just to be certain that God heard me: "God, make Yourself real to me."

> "This is the assurance we have in approaching God:
> that if we ask anything according to his will, he hears
> us. And if we know that he hears us - whatever we
> ask – we know that we have what we asked of him"
> —1 John 5:14-15 (NIV)

## Honesty is God's Best Policy

It was early one morning several months after my conversion when my wife, Bimini, told me that as a girl she had dreamed of the kind of man she would marry. She also said that after our first ten years together, she knew I wasn't that man. But she went on to say that since I had surrendered my life to Jesus, I was now everything and more than she had ever imagined. Well, on that morning and after sixteen years of marriage, as we lay there in bed praising God for all He had done, my wife finally popped the question that had always terrified me. She asked me straight away, "Have you ever cheated on me?" At that moment, the Holy Spirit spoke to my heart for the first time and said, "*Tony, you have one shot at this. You have lied to everyone in your life for forty-six years. You don't even remember what truth is. I can clear the slate today and allow the healing to begin if you'll just be honest for the first time in your life. Right now, you need to tell her everything!*"

I thought to myself, "Everything?"

The Lord confirmed, "*Everything!*"

I knew at that moment that I was not only about to lose my wife, I was going to lose my children, too. I remember a supernatural peace washed over me and I decided to just trust God! That morning, I cleaned out the closest and revealed every dirty secret of my life: the prostitutes, pornography, mistresses, drug addictions, gambling—everything. I didn't hold one thing back and in the process of all my transparentcy, I ripped my wife's heart out. She had no idea the man she had been married to for the past sixteen years, but God knew that she was spiritually strong enough to hear the truth. That truth would set us both free from the grip of Satan so God could be glorified in His covenant of marriage.

"Put to death, therefore, whatever belongs to your earthly nature: sexual immorality, impurity, lust, evil desires and greed, which is idolatry. Because of these, the wrath of God is coming. You used to walk in these ways, in the life you once

lived. But now you must rid yourselves of all such things as
these: anger, rage, malice, slander, and filthy language from
your lips. Do not lie to each other, since you have taken off your
old self with its practices and have put on the new self, which
is being renewed in knowledge in the image of its Creator."
—Colossians 3:5-10 (NIV)

## Weekend to Remember God

Again, in God's divine plan, my wife had signed us up for a Christian
couples getaway at church. Again, I had an exit strategy already
prepared. Still feeling the wake of the closet cleaning experience
just a week prior, the roles were reversed for this weekend outing. I
didn't need an exit strategy. I needed a miracle from God to convince
my wife to go with me to this "Weekend to Remember" Christian
couples getaway.

My wife loved the new man that God had been transforming
since March 13, 2008, but she hated the old sinful man she thought
she once knew. I simply asked her if she would join the new man for
a weekend of healing and renewing, leaving all the consequences up
to God. God truly breathed upon this weekend — the love letters,
the date night on the premiere weekend of the movie *Fireproof*, and a
special book annomously given to us called *The Love Dare*. It was all
too perfect to be anything other than God's sovereign hand upon us.
Our marriage was brought into oneness with Christ. Its restoration
began to exemplify the fullness and richness of the eternal covenant
in Christ to which we had committed sixteen years prior, but had
never experienced.

"Husbands, love your wives, just as Christ loved the church and
gave himself up for her to make her holy, cleansing her by the
washing with water through the word, and to present her to
himself as a radiant church, without stain or wrinkle or any other
blemish, but holy and blameless. In this same way, husbands ought

to love their wives as their own bodies. He who loves his wife loves himself. After all, no one ever hated his own body, but he feeds and cares for it, just as Christ does the church –for we are members of his body. "For this reason a man will leave his father and mother and be united to his wife, and the two will become one flesh." This is a profound mystery – but I am talking about Christ and the church. However, each one of you also must love his wife as he loves himself, and the wife must respect her husband."
—Ephesians 5:25-33 (NIV)

"From him the whole body, joined and held together by every supporting ligament, grows and builds itself up in love, as each part does its work. So I tell you this, and insist on it in the Lord, that you must no longer live as the Gentiles do, in the futility of their thinking. They are darkened in their understanding and separated from the life of God because of the ignorance that is in them due to the hardening of their hearts. Having lost all sensitivity, they have given themselves over to sensuality so as to indulge in every kind of impurity, with a continual lust for more. "You, however, did not come to know Christ that way. Surely you heard of him and were taught in him in accordance with the truth that is in Jesus. You were taught, with regard to your former way of life, to put off your old self, which is being corrupted by its deceitful desires; to be made new in the attitude of your minds; and to put on the new self, created to be like God in true righteousness and holiness."
—Ephesians 4:16-24 (NIV)

"For we know that our old self was crucified with him so that the body of sin might be rendered powerless, that we should no longer be slaves to sin — because anyone who has died has been freed from sin. Now if we died with Christ, we believe that we will also live with him. For we know that since Christ was raised from the dead, he cannot die again; death no longer has mastery over him. The death he died, he died to sin once for all; but the

life he lives, he lives to God. In the same way, count yourselves dead to sin but alive to God in Christ Jesus. Therefore do not let sin reign in your mortal body so that you obey its evil desires. Do not offer the parts of your body to sin, as instruments of wickedness, but rather offer yourselves to God, as those who have been brought from death to life; and offer the parts of your body to him as instruments of righteousness. For sin shall not be your master, because you are not under law, but under grace."
—Romans 6:6-14 (NIV)

## My Resource Center

God had been completely transforming my life. It was overwhelming. There were still many uncertainties standing between me and my Savior. God was revealing all the poison and corruption I had built into my company. The resource center that helped fund all the things the old man once desired, the same things the new man despised. Once again, my wonderful wife had signed us up for another one of these Christian conferences. It was a financial peace gig led by a guy named Dave. I went just because the guy was a Christian.

I watched Dave on stage, talking about managing the resources with which God has entrusted us. I remember thinking, "wow, this is what it's all about." He gave one biblical account after another of how we are called to be good stewards over our greenbacks—and that it all belonged to God. Not just ten percent. I was blown away by his teaching about handling personal finances and his sensible action plan for living a debt-free life. At the end, Dave called business owners to the stage and told us about his one-week intensive business seminar in Cancun, Mexico, where he would share similar biblical values, but apply them to our business as well as our personal finances to help us obtain financial peace. The seminar was for training in entrepreneurial leadership within our businesses.

My wife and I attended the event that November. The one-on-one time my wife and I spent with Dave, his wife Sharon, and their kids, and his team was beyond measuring. It was a God-given opportunity to be mentored by this man. Through his own testimony, Dave gave me the ingredients and a launching platform to build a Christian foundation for Ground Zero Electrostatics. He helped me see the commonalities between a static control business and the Kingdom of God.

"For by him all things were created: things in heaven and on earth, visible and invisible, whether thrones or powers or rulers or authorities; all things were created by him and for him."
—Colossians 1:16 (NIV)

## His Ministry

Dave and the entrepreneurial leadership program gave us the concrete and rebar required to pour a Christian foundation which has produced much fruit for the Kingdom. Then God began to reveal what it looked like for static control and the Kingdom of God to come together. God had blessed us with a solid foundation, but we had no framework and not enough intentional Christian call-to-action. That's when a group called C-12 came into my life. "It sounds explosive! What is it and is it better than C-4?" I asked one business consultant from Chicago.

His response was, "It's a Christian organization made up of local Christian CEOs, presidents and business owners. It's a group of peer-to-peer accountability partners that meet once a month as an acting board of directors and/or advisors." After the fourth time God put C-12 in my path through non-related people, I finally wised up, submitted to His calling, and joined the group one week later.

C-12 was the necessary framework, the Christian call-to-action, the wise counsel, and the conduit that God knew I needed to weather the storms ahead. C-12 was the voice of God's wisdom that helped me realize that Ground Zero wasn't my company at all—it was God's company. It's the for-profit ministry and the platform with which He blessed me to give Jesus away and advance the Kingdom. It's the marketplace ministry He intended me to use for His glory and the divine purpose and calling on my life… in this season, anyway.

"For I know the plans I have for you,' declares
the Lord, 'plans to prosper you and not to harm
you, plans to give you hope and a future."
—Jeremiah 29:11 (NIV)

"For where two or three come together in
my name, there am I with them."
—Matthew 18:20 (NIV)

"Plans fail for lack of counsel, but with many advisers they succeed."
—Proverbs 15:22 (NIV)

"For lack of guidance a nation falls, but
many advisers make victory sure."
—Proverbs 11:14 (NIV)

"An honest answer is like a kiss on the lips."
—Proverbs 24:26 (NIV)

"There is a time for everything, and a season
for every activity under heaven."
—Ecclesiastes 3:1 (NIV)

## Waiting Through the Storms

By allowing God to guide me through practicing His presence, and by following and implementing the wise counsel shared by my brothers in Christ at C-12, He was preparing me for uncharted waters, times of the rockiest, most barren terrain imaginable, with rough seas that would make the perfect storm look like a clearing shower. If someone could have given me a glimpse of my future, I couldn't have imagined the series of trials and tests that God was about to allow in my life. It was His refining fire.

"But now, this is what the LORD says — he who created you, O Jacob, he who formed you, O Israel: 'Fear not, for I have redeemed you; I have called you by name; you are mine. When you pass through the waters, I will be with you; and when you pass through the rivers, they will not sweep over you. When you walk through the fire, you will not be burned; the flames will not set you ablaze. For I am the LORD, your God, the Holy One of Israel, your Savior; I give Egypt for your ransom, Cush and Seba in your stead.'"
—Isaiah 43:1-3 (NIV)

"Be joyful in hope, patient in affliction, faithful in prayer."
—Romans 12:12 (NIV)

"Consider it pure joy, my brothers, whenever you face trials of many kinds"
—James 1:2 (NIV)

"Be strong and courageous. Do not be afraid or terrified because of them, for the LORD your God goes with you; he will never leave you nor forsake you."
—Deuteronomy 31:6 (NIV)

## From Heros to Zeros

As a company, we went from heroes (knocking down $125,000/ week) to zeros (clawing to muster up a $30,000/month). It happened overnight. The business dried up before my very eyes. The harder I tried, the worse things became. I lost eighty percent of our workforce and our bank reserves plummeted to the point of financial collapse. There were many weeks when we couldn't make payroll. Even when we could, it was always prioritized from staff to owners, which never went well on the homefront.

I didn't get it. God had completely consumed me for the past twelve months and I felt like I was walking on clouds. Now I was asking myself, "Where did God go and who flipped the off switch on *my business?*" There lay the problem: *"my business."* I was still putting the business before God. There was still too much of *"me"* in the picture. I was holding on too tightly and trying too hard. This process took me from a prideful business owner to a humble servant and a trusted steward of the Kingdom.

> "Have mercy on me, O God, have mercy on me, for
> in you my soul takes refuge. I will take refuge in the
> shadow of your wings until the disaster has passed."
> —Psalm 57:1 (NIV)

> "But he said to me, 'My grace is sufficient for you,
> for my power is made perfect in weakness.'"
> —2 Corinthians 12:9 (NIV)

## God's Yoke Revealed

Humility wasn't the only treasure in these trials. At this point in my journey, I plugged myself into every Bible study and men's group I could find. During one of my 4:00 a.m. Bible studies with a group of 4:59 a.m. Jesus freaks, my redneck cousin, Skipper, had shared a message about the "Yoke of Jesus." I didn't have a clue what this meant, but God laid it on my heart to have a deeper understanding of what this 'yoke' looked like. It wasn't an egg, I can assure you of that.

Once I understood what a yoke was, God revealed His yoke to me. I must say that it felt weird the first day I took on the yoke of Christ around my neck. I felt guilty because I was no longer driving the bus but was now a precious passenger, responsible to see that the right team members were aboard — nothing more. It seemed too easy. I wasn't working hard, and it just seemed to free me of some heavy burdens I'd been schlepping around for years.

This revelation came to me during quiet time one morning: I was no longer in charge of my life or responsible for finding a solution to our financial dilemma ... He was. I was to wait patiently on God and trust that He cares and is in control. *Trusting versus trying.* Now there was a concept that would lead to growing my faith by leaps and bounds. His business, not mine. Could it really be all about God? God in control, not me? He is my provider and I am His child? Wow. Could it be about Him guiding and me believing and trusting in Him for everything? This was a radical reality and it is exactly what it all meant.

"All things have been committed to me by my Father.
No one knows the Son except the Father, and no one
knows the Father except the Son and those to whom
the Son chooses to reveal him. Come to me, all you who
are weary and burdened, and I will give you rest."
—Matthew 11:27-28 (NIV)

"He will have no fear of bad news; his heart
is steadfast, trusting in the LORD."
—Psalm 112:7 (NIV)

"Am I trying to win the approval of men, or of God?
Or am I trying to please men? If I were still trying to
please men, I would not be a servant of Christ."
—Galatians 1:10 (NIV)

## Trial by Fire

I resigned as CEO and signed on as a servant leader. I was broke and broken. God had stripped me and His company of everything and He began to turn up the heat at the office! With one or two lawsuits coming in every week, and with collection calls and sales opportunities at a ratio of 3:1, we were beaten down and feeling beyond helpless and hopeless.

Paychecks were scarce. Commissions were non-existent and we were in a survival mode that made *Naked and Afraid* look like *Disney's Fort Wilderness*. It was this way for months, although personally, my wife and I had never been happier in our new joy-filled relationship with Christ. Then He turned up the heat on the homefront.

It started with the A.T.M. spitting out a ridiculous piece of white paper instead of the green bills to which I had grown accustomed. Nonsuffcient funds. I thought to myself, "What in the world is wrong with this silly machine?" I rushed to work, to confirm with my bank that this was a case of fraud or stolen identity. Well, it wasn't fraud, and it wasn't the A.T.M. It was another three letter acronym, the I.R.S. They had just frozen all our assets and cleaned out our entire savings, my retirement, and every penny in our personal checking account. Things were going from bad to much worse.

"In this you greatly rejoice, though now for a little while you may
have had to suffer grief in all kinds of trials. These have come
so that your faith – of greater worth than gold, which perishes
even though refined by fire – may be proved genuine and may
result in praise, glory and honor when Christ is revealed."
—1 Peter 1:6-7 (NIV)

"And the God of all grace, who called you to his eternal glory
in Christ, after you have suffered a little while, will himself
restore you and make you strong, firm and steadfast."
—1 Peter 5:10 (NIV)

"Consider it pure joy, my brothers, whenever you face trials of
many kinds, because you know that the testing of your faith

develops perseverance. Perseverance must finish its work so that you may be mature and complete, not lacking anything."
—James 1:2-4 (NIV)

"I have told you these things so that in me you may have peace. In this world you will have trouble. But take heart! I have overcome the world."
—John 16:33 (NIV)

## Backup Plan

We met with our corporate attorney to discuss a strategy to deal with the lawsuits that required our responses. Our plan was a common secular approach in business today, for people under the pressure of the world who don't know the source of their security: bankruptcy. I kept thinking to myself, "Just walk away from all your troubles. What in the world are you waiting for? File already." Our attorney's plan was brilliant and I agreed to the conception of a new corporation in my wife's name, hanging all our creditors out to dry in order to regain control of my life and His business. I should have felt great about this, right? Wrong. I had a pit in my stomach the size of a peach and an uneasiness as I thought to myself, "We drafted a wonderful and well thought-out business strategy. Just be happy in it."

I knew I would feel better if I would speak to God. I sat in my truck in front of my attorney's office and shared the depths of my heart with our Lord. I told Him how fearful I was and when I looked up, I saw on my rearview mirror the florescent purple sticky note that had been staring me in the face for months. It was the address to a Bible study in downtown Bradenton. I had been invited months ago. Coincidence, I guess. It was only a block away, right around the corner from where I sat crying out to God.

I walked into a group of smiling business men and introduced myself. We watched a video about faith. The storyline was about Abraham walking with God, assuring him that he would be blessed with a son from his own seed. He would have as many descendants as the stars above and many nations would rise up from his seed. Abraham and Sarah weren't getting any younger as they were pushing upward towards one hundred years old. So they implemented a backup plan with their servant Hagar, just in case God's promise didn't come to fruition.

I immediately knew what I had done and why I had that pit in my stomach. I had created my own backup plan, just in case God's plan didn't work out. Oh, Tony of little faith! I asked these new brothers in Christ to stop the video. Then I shared my conviction from Holy Spirit and asked to be excused long enough to call my attorney with the news that we were not going to file for bankruptcy. Instead, we were going to wait on God to either show up and deliver us or move us into greener pastures—His best things for my life. I think my attorney wanted to recommend a good psychiatrist, as this choice would have a rippling effect on many people.

"Now faith is being sure of what we hope for
and certain of what we do not see."
—Hebrews 11:1 (NIV)

"...for everyone born of God overcomes the world. This is
the victory that has overcome the world, even our faith."
—1 John 5:4 (NIV)

"Let those who fear the LORD say: 'His love endures forever.' In my anguish I cried to the LORD, and he answered by setting me free. The LORD is with me; I will not be afraid. What can man do to me? The LORD is with me; he is my helper. I will look in triumph on my enemies. It is better to take refuge in the LORD than to trust in man. It is better to take refuge in the LORD than to trust in princes. All the nations surrounded me, but in the name of the LORD I cut them off. They surrounded me on every side, but in the name of the LORD I cut them off. They

swarmed around me like bees, but they died out as quickly as burning thorns; in the name of the LORD I cut them off. I was pushed back and about to fall, but the LORD helped me. The LORD is my strength and my song; he has become my salvation."
—Psalm 118:4-14 (NIV)

## The Jesus Inbox

God keeps reminding me of *George Mueller's* contagious and freeing statement of faith: "I will always have all I need to do all God asks of me." Our finance manager and I were sitting in our typical Wednesday morning finance meeting, which never took much of our time back then. As we finished up in prayer, we were both in tears over our abundance of financial trauma. Then, in the moment, God put it on my heart to create a sticker labeled *"Jesus."* I asked my finance manager to affix the Jesus label to one of the inbound correspondence boxes we all used to circulate important documents. Since Jesus was our new CEO and there had always been an empty correspondence box at the top, we were obedient to His request and the "Jesus inbox" was born.

In place of tears from all the financial threats that poured in on a daily basis, we would simply place in the "Jesus inbox" all financial threats and issues that were bigger than we were and around which it was flat-out impossible for us to wrap our finite minds. It was twelve inches thick and jam-packed. This was several years ago. Today the box holds only prayers and praises. There is a remnant of debt still out there, but it is being paid back at an accelerated rate as God wills and provides faithfully and abundantly. God has poured His Grace upon all the threats and His company is getting healthier with each and every breath He so divinely provides.

> "Jesus looked at them and said, 'With man this is impossible, but with God all things are possible.'"
> —Matthew 19:26 (NIV)

"Trust in the Lord with all your heart and lean not on
your own understanding; in all your ways acknowledge
him and he will make your paths straight."
—Proverbs 3:5-6 (NIV)

"'Have faith in God,' Jesus answered. 'I tell you the truth,
if anyone says to this mountain, 'Go, throw yourself into
the sea,' and does not doubt in his heart but believes that
what he says will happen, it will be done for him."
—Mark 11:22-23 (NIV)

## Blinded Bankers

I can describe the following only as God's divine plan and another
miracle from our Savior. In April 2009, the bank which held our
maxed-out line of credit called me in for a meeting; or rather, an
ambush. The meeting wasn't exclusively with my banker, as I was
told. It was actually with the banker, along with a loan committee.
And they wanted answers.

Their biggest questions were, "Do you know why we have asked
you here today?" "How in the world are you going to pay the money
you owe us?" and "Anthony, what are you doing to stop the bleeding
and fix the business?"

I replied with a bold and excited, "We're praying." As they all
stared at me (as if I were a green alien from Mars) and then looked
at one another, I realized I had failed their first line of questioning.

When the regional vice president replied, "Seriously, Anthony!"

I rebutted, "I am being quite serious! We begin each day in prayer
and give thanks at the closing of each day. We pray with our customers
and vendors. We even have weekly Bible studies at the office. I have
backed down as CEO and taken on the position of servant leader."

"Who is actually running the day-to-day business affairs of the
company?" asked the assets manager, with some irritability.

"We have elected God to step in as active CEO." I saw their faces. "Oh boy. This isn't going well," I thought to myself.

"But what are you doing to get the business in order? We can't figure out by your financials how you are still in business. You look insolvent."

"We are working diligently on right-sizing the business." I said. "I have laid off ninety percent of the staff, including my mother, father, and brother. We are doing all the difficult things. I have had to endure tough circumstances these past months and I am thankful we don't have brown paper up in our windows, like so many of our neighbors. We are still here." I assured them we were still the $5 to $6 million dollar per year company we were two years prior. I told them we were keeping our hands and feet busy for Christ and that I felt confident we would have a profitable June.

The asset manager responded, "How do you know you will have a profitable June? Do you have a crystal ball, Anthony?"

"No. Definitely not. Neither do the banks. Didn't you all just get bailed out for $750 billion dollars? Nobody saw that coming!"

The regional vice president stood up and said he was curious to see the outcome of my confidence. He said he had taken part in more of these types of meetings than he cared to admit, but this was by far the strangest one yet! In his opinion, we wouldn't make it through the remainder of the month of April, let alone June. His point was that we were clearly insolvent and incapable of recovering. He went on to say that he wasn't sure about the whole "God and praying thing," but that he would allow us the two months until June to show significant change and prove our profitability, before he pulled the plug.

"If the world hates you, keep in mind that it hated me first. If you belonged to the world, it would love you as its own. As it is, you do not belong to the world, but I have chosen you out of the world. That is why the world hates you. Remember the words I spoke to you: 'No servant is greater than his

master.' If they persecuted me, they will persecute you also.
If they obeyed my teaching, they will obey yours also."
—John 15:18-20 (NIV)

"Who shall separate us from the love of Christ? Shall trouble
or hardship or persecution or famine or nakedness or danger or
sword? As it is written: 'For your sake we face death all day long;
we are considered as sheep to be slaughtered.' No, in all these
things we are more than conquerors through him who loved us.
For I am convinced that neither death nor life, neither angels nor
demons, neither the present nor the future, nor any powers, neither
height nor depth, nor anything else in all creation, will be able to
separate us from the love of God that is in Christ Jesus our Lord."
—Romans 8:35-39 (NIV)

"The LORD is my light and my salvation – whom shall I fear? The
LORD is the stronghold of my life – of whom shall I be afraid?"
—Psalm 27:1 (NIV)

## God's Companies Are Resilient

We did lose $180,000 the first quarter of 2009, and $89,000 in April,
but we only lost $3,000 in May and ended up showing a $3,000 dollar
profit by June. By God's good grace, Ground Zero Electrostatics
has been profitable almost every month since. I praise Him that we
haven't missed a payroll since the first quarter of 2009. That is over
seven years ago. At the current rate the Lord is pouring out His
abundance and blessing upon us, we will soon be a debt-free company
once again.

These things can be explained only by the holy power of Jesus
Christ Almighty. The last words from our banker were, "I wanted to
tell you guys how happy I am to see this has all turned around for you.
Keep up the effort and keep talking to the Man in the sky. He seems
to have a great impact on all of us." Our banker has since inquired

about our Thursday Bible study on more than one occasion, and even attended once or twice. Praise the Lord for the things He has done, all He is doing and all He will continue to do in the future.

"...so is my word that goes out from my mouth: It will
not return to me empty, but will accomplish what I
desire and achieve the purpose for which I sent it."
—Isaiah 55:11 (NIV)

"But seek first his kingdom and his righteousness,
and all these things will be given to you as well."
—Matthew 6:33 (NIV)

## God's in the Static Control Business

We have made the decision to continue giving our Lord the first ten percent of all gross profits that come into His storehouse. Once our debt is paid in full and we are no longer enslaved to the lender, ninety percent of His company profits will be utilized for Kingdom-building opportunities as He guides our path. He has been doing amazing things through this generosity culture that we adopted back in November, 2008, and we are constantly watching for every opportunity and the good works in which He has prepared for us to walk. The old "resource center" that was once used for my personal worldly pleasures and Satan's success has been transformed into a profit center for the Kingdom work of Jesus Christ Almighty, our Lord and Savior, to whom we are thankful.

"And my God will meet all your needs according
to his glorious riches in Christ Jesus."
—Philippians 4:19 (NIV)

"Now to him who is able to do immeasurably more than all
we ask or imagine, according to his power that is at work

within us, to him be glory in the church and in Christ Jesus throughout all generations, for ever and ever! Amen."
—Ephesians 3:20-21 (NIV)

I could go on bragging on my Abba Papa, relating God-encounters and testifying to miracle after miracle Jesus has done in my life beyond those first two years after I met Him face-to-face on my living room floor. Who knows? Maybe the accounts of the past five years of His life in me will be in the next writing He anoints and guides me to share.

This journey has been amazing. He has used an uneducated, simple-minded man and his testimony to lead others to Christ, to encourage the hopeless, to mend the hearts of the broken, and to lead His lost sheep back into the loving arms of their Shepherd. I can testify that we serve a star-breathing, heart-transforming, mind-restoring, faithful God that is our endless source and supply of acceptance, significance, purpose, value, love, joy, peace, strength, courage, kindness, goodness, and every attribute that is desirable now and on into eternity.

I have complete victory and freedom in Christ, through claiming the full inheritance that I have in Jesus, who has become my life, and through believing in His amazing grace. I no longer desire anything in this world through which we now pass, except for the relationships He will surely allow to develop around me and through me while I give away His good news and His awaiting abundance: life for the world that has rejected Him, but which He so loves!

I Love You, Heavenly Father, Lord Jesus, and almighty Holy Spirit.

# CHAPTER 3

## A Rebellious Father and His Outlaw Son

In 2006, I had sent a team of flooring mechanics to install a high-tech static control floor for an electronics company in Nada, Oklahoma. Zack was the newest member of our installation team, and he had an amazing story. A country boy from Iowa, he had been reared by his mother until she could no longer control him or deal with his destructive behavior. He had a host of behavioral issues growing up, most of which, I believe, stemmed from the absence of his father's love and discipline. Zack, like many today, grew up in the midst of divorce, broken and dysfunctional relationships, as well as constant exposure to a lifestyle of drug abuse and addiction.

> "As for you, you were dead in your transgressions and sins,
> in which you used to live when you followed the ways of this
> world and of the ruler of the kingdom of the air, the spirit
> who is now at work in those who are disobedient. All of us
> also lived among them at one time, gratifying the cravings
> of our sinful nature and following its desires and thoughts.
> Like the rest, we were by nature objects of wrath."
> —Ephesians 2:1-3 (NIV)

Zack had walked away from most of this when we hired him. He had been clean of drugs and sober of alcohol for a year and had begun a new start on life with his estranged father in Florida. All in all, Zack was a great kid who never stood a chance at life because he was influenced and overshadowed by the lives his parents lived.

At that point in time, neither Zack nor his father realized that life can be found only in the person of Jesus Christ. They were clueless that our true identity, the fullness of our inheritance, our divine purpose and destiny for living was established long before, "in the beginning." They were completely blinded from the truth that the veil in the temple had been torn from top to bottom and all these things could be made known to them through the greatest gift ever given! They were sightless to the fact that life is given in the form of a gift. It needs only to be received. This was a story foreign to both father and son.

> "And this is the testimony: God has given us eternal life,
> and this life is in his Son. He who has the Son has life; he
> who does not have the Son of God does not have life."
> —1 John 5:11-12 (NIV)

"Praise be to the God and Father of our Lord Jesus Christ, who has blessed us in the heavenly realms with every spiritual blessing in Christ. For he chose us in him before the creation of the world to be holy and blameless in his sight. In love he predestined us to be adopted as his sons through Jesus Christ in accordance with his pleasure and will — to the praise of his glorious grace, which he has freely given us in the One he loves. In him we have redemption through his blood, the forgiveness of sins, in accordance with the riches of God's grace that he lavished on us with all wisdom and understanding. And he made known to us the mystery of his will according to his good pleasure, which he purposed in Christ, to be put into effect when the times will have reached their fulfillment — to bring all things in heaven and on earth together under one head, even Christ. In him we were also chosen, having been predestined according to the plan of him who works out everything in conformity with the purpose of his will, in order that we, who

were the first to hope in Christ, might be for the praise of his glory. And you also were included in Christ when you heard the word of truth, the gospel of your salvation. Having believed, you were marked in him with a seal, the promised Holy Spirit, who is a deposit guaranteeing our inheritance until the redemption of those who are God's possession — to the praise of his glory."
—Ephesians 1:3-14 (NIV)

Shortly after Zack arrived in Nada, he started using methamphetamines again and never returned home to his father. He called from the Tomahawk County Jail, saying he had been set up by the Nada, Oklahoma, police department, who had planted drugs on him. His father thought the story was unlikely. Unexpectedly however, Zack was released. The substance found under the back seat of the police car, which they claimed was his, was not an illegal, controlled substance. It was, rather, silica salts. Maybe there was truth to Zack's story.

Zack was found innocent on this charge, but events over the next six months led to his second incarceration. A woman saw Zack steal her purse from the front seat of her van, which was parked in front of a school in Nada. As he drove away, she chased him down and jumped in through the open window, determined to pull his keys from the ignition. In the struggle, she fell back out of the car and as Zack fled, her hand was crushed by the rear tire of his car.

The woman was rushed to the area hospital. Doctors noted bad bruising but thankfully, found no broken or fractured bones. She demanded a second opinion and to be airlifted to Oklahoma City, where it was confirmed that she had sustained no permanent damage, no broken bones. The Nada police, however, told Zack that the woman he ran over was air-flighted to Oklahoma City and was fighting for her life. He faced charges for robbery by force and fear, assault with a deadly weapon, destruction of city property (for kicking out the back windshield of the police cruiser) and several other lesser charges, such as eluding and resisting. Zack feared for his life, for the loss of his new start, and his career opportunity with Ground Zero, but mostly, I think, he feared how it would impact his newly restored relationship with his father.

Zack's dad was crushed, but chose to help his son, who he felt he had abandoned so many years before. If he had been there for the early years of his son's life, would things be different now? Maybe Zack would not be facing the next fifteen years of his life behind prison bars.

Zack's father hired one of those high-powered, go-for-the-jugular attorneys who promised the world and said he could get all these trumped-up charges reduced to what they actually were: petty larceny for the eight dollars he had ripped off from the seat of an unoccupied vehicle, fleeing a crime scene, destruction of city property and resisting arrest. Zack would serve two years in prison and then one year in a drug treatment program on a work release basis, as a worse case scenario. This sounded good to both Zack and his dad, but neither were prepared for how this story would unfold and begin to reveal the corruption behind those jailhouse walls.

Why didn't Zack's father just walk away? Why didn't Ground Zero Electronics fire this kid and move on? The answer is simple. Zack is my only begotten, always-being-loved son in whom I will never give up on again, and I am the lost-and-found son of a lost-and-found son of the Father's Saving Son.

# CHAPTER 4

# Divine Intervention Between
# the Father and His Sons

It was 2009, over two years since I had last seen Zack. His newly appointed Public Defender told me that I would not be permitted to see my son if I chose to fly up from Florida for his arraignment. However, I knew what God had told me, so I asked if I could come just the same, and he hesitantly agreed. I don't think he could imagine why I would want to fly all the way up to Oklahoma, to see Zack only from across a courtroom for a few fleeting moments.

As I watched that chain of broken, hopeless faces march single file into the courtroom, all shackled together and dressed in fluorescent orange jumpsuits, my heart pounding in the depths of my chest. Then I saw him, my precious boy. Zackery had entered the courtroom and our eyes met, a bright and hopeful smile lit up upon his face. A gladness to see his father for the first time in over two years, and for the first time since his father had entered into a born-again relationship with Jesus Christ.

Although Zack wore that courageous smile, it couldn't begin to hide those hurting fearful eyes that never seemed able to hide the lie within. Zack's public defender quickly acknowledged that I was there with a brief introduction and a consoling, "As I told you over the telephone, Mr. Murfin, you won't be able to see your son, Zackery, today other than from across this room. I'm not sure how today will go, but he should receive his sentencing this morning."

I replied, "I am blessed just to see my son's face, even if it's from across this courtroom. It has been so long since I've seen Zack's infectious smile that it, in and of itself, made the entire journey well worthwhile."

The bailiff called the courtroom to order and the judge quickly called Zack's attorney to approach the bench. They conversed a few moments. Then the judge looked at me, in the front row, weeping to God for His mercy and favor over my son's future and soul.

> "For I know the plans I have for you,' declares
> the Lord, 'plans to prosper you and not to harm
> you, plans to give you hope and a future."
> —Jeremiah 29:11 (NIV)

The judge spoke again to Zack's public defender, who then walked directly over to me. He explained that Zack's sentencing had been postponed and set for another day. With great disappointment in my heart, but also a sense of relief, I heard the public defender say the judge was allowing me five minutes with Zack in his private chambers. This was the first of many times God would divinely make a way for a father to express his love for his son.

It felt like the sweetest and shortest five minutes I had ever experienced! Zack had so many questions, so much to say as he threw his handcuffed arms around me and lifted me up into the chest of his six foot, four inch frame. He told me how much he loved me, missed me, and how sorry he was for the trouble he had caused. I quickly shushed him and began to tell the truth God had revealed to me about Himself since my conversion and adoption into the Kingdom. Zack said, "I know, Dad. Something about you is so very different. I could hear it in all those letters you wrote about finding Jesus and about how God freed you from all those things I never knew about you. That's crazy stuff, Dad. I want to know and learn about Jesus like you did. Dad, I want to learn about Him from you."

Zack then shared, "You know that jailer who led me into the courtroom, Dad? Well, he put me in here." I quickly ushered Zack back to the fact that it was his own choosing that put him where he was. With a repentant heart, he came into alignment with God's truth and began to understand that blame and denial are a dead-end road and remnants of the fall of mankind.

> "The man said, 'The woman you put here with me — she
> gave me some fruit from the tree, and I ate it.' Then the
> Lord God said to the woman, 'What is this you have done?'
> The woman said, 'The serpent deceived me, and I ate.'"
> —Genesis 3:12-13 (NIV)

CHAPTER 5

# A Hardened Heart Softened by God

Our five minutes was like a vapor and we were escorted back into the courtroom. Shortly after, I watched as those bright orange jumpers paraded back out of the courtroom. I looked into Zack's eyes as he walked past me and he began to cry. I immediately began to pray and tear up again. Then, God did the unimaginable.

I watched as Zack disappeared from my sight and until all that orange had faded away. Then the jailer turned to me, "Do you want to spend some time with your son? I don't know why you would want to spend time with this kid, but if you do, then come follow me." This was the man, Zack had said, who had put him in prison.

I jumped to my feet. As we walked, the jailer explained, "There is no visitation for inmates who are held over before being transferred back to their prisons. There is no visitation on weekdays — no exceptions. Also, you must have prior written approval and an inmate request form. I felt that I needed to make an exception for you, since you came all the way from Florida."

He locked us up in a wet, cold cell of the condemned and corrupt Tomahawk County Jail. It's such a bad place that it has left a wake of history behind it, including, but not limited to, John Grishum's New York Times Bestseller, *The Innocent Dude*. This book confirms the corruption within the Tomahawk County criminal justice system in little Nada, Oklahoma. A father and his son were locked up in a jail cell for five hours together, but I was the most joyful man to ever sit behind jailhouse bars, having and holding my precious boy, sharing life together as I gave away Christ within me, the hope of glory.

Zackery began to share his heart about all the wrong he had done and how he regretted the poor choices he'd made. He was remorseful for backsliding into his old addiction to crystal meth and for the harm he brought to the woman he ran over, and the pain he caused her family.

Then Zack said, "If these walls could talk," and began to reveal what went on behind the walls and bars of this viperous pit. Its darkness and deception was far beyond my imagination. Its corruption echoed its way through the criminal justice system of this little town in the middle of nowhere-ville. It opened my eyes to how dispirited and fallen this world really is.

While Zack was serving his original sentence, his attorney got his time reduced to a two-year prison sentence plus one year in a supervised drug treatment program. This was in exchange for Zack's guilty plea and with the condition that he not get into any more trouble. But things had taken a drastic turn, a downward spiral that got worse beyond our imagination.

Zack told me how a riot had broken out after a 9 millimeter pistol was discovered in an inmate's mattress. I don't understand how this happens in a secure law enforcement facility, but it was obvious that poor choices were made on both sides of the law. I couldn't believe the corruption within this little jailhouse.

In the midst of this riot, and with the aid of two other inmates, Zack was captured on video surveillance as he ignited a wad of paper towels which had been stuffed inside a flameproof mattress. For this, a charge of 20 years for felony arson was added to Zackery's two-year sentence.

Prison authorities manipulated and threatened Zack during their investigation. They told him they would reactivate all his original charges and run them consecutively. He'd be locked up for the next 50-75 years if he didn't plead guilty to the felony arson charge and waive his rights for a preliminary hearing. Felony arson is considered an 85 percent violent offence, which means 85 percent of his time must be served and is not impacted by good time or early parole.

# CHAPTER 6

## God Doesn't Waste Anything!

As we brought all this into God's light, Zack asked me to elaborate on my encounter with God in all the letters I had been writing him for many months. As we talked about all Jesus had done in my life, I shared God's full testimony. Zack asked, "Who are you and what have you done with my dad?"

Zack began to realize that the only difference between him and what he thought to be his all-together dad was that his dad never got caught. His dad had been living out of the same shadows of brokenness, the same identity crisis, the same lies, the same guilt, the same shame and the same rejection for years, except he was better at hiding it. This is the de-generational perversion of a son from the seed of Adam rearing a son of the seed of Adam. A prodigal of a prodigal.

God's testimony for my life was so real to Zack that he said, "Dad, I want what you have. I want to learn about Jesus, just like you did. Will you teach me about Jesus?" Zack fell into my arms as surrendered as anyone I have ever known, and God used me to lead my precious lost son into the loving arms of his originally-intended birthright and eternal God-given heritage — Zack in Jesus Christ Almighty. Wow. Praise the Lord.

# CHAPTER 7

# The Epistle of a Father's Abraham-Isaac Moment

This story within a story is one of the most difficult storms I have ever navigated as a father or as a man. It was a battle of the forces of death and darkness against the forces of life and light, good against evil, the truth versus a lie. It was a battle for the souls of both a father and a son; a battle that deceived and divided the mind between what is right and what is wrong. It required a choice between trusting in the self-life and what is seen in the fallen realm or trusting in the Christ-life and what is unseen, in the realm of truth and the everlasting.

This story sits in the midst of my utter transparency with a band of brothers called *Wildmen*. God had allowed me to share life with these men as a poured-out expression of His love in a small-group setting.

I had been teaching this group of men what God had been teaching me about a life in grace. I shared with these beloved men the following letter about the good, the bad, and the ugly of the victorious Christian life as I walked it out. It's certainly not always bouquets and butterflies.

*Good Afternoon, Wildmen Brothers:*
*I just wanted to take a minute this morning and tell each one of you how regretful I am that I missed Wildmen and our meeting last Tuesday night.*

*For me it's a joy and privilege to be able to join with you guys each Tuesday as we come together in union, being built up as one body to explore our true identities in Christ. It is truly a blessing to watch and share the realities of our Almighty Father God unfold and come alive in each of our lives, as His truths are brought into the light and sown into the depths of our souls by the Holy Spirit. It is amazing to be able to hear and see how God is uniquely and independently shaping, forming and bringing each of us into the likeness of His Glorious Son, Jesus.*

*Also, being able to corporately experience and celebrate these victories in Christ as a band of brothers who are being stripped of our worldly exteriors to see our loving Savior shining through the very men He created each one of us to be — that's incredible. We are His masterpieces in the making.*

"For we are God's workmanship, created in Christ Jesus to do good works, which God prepared in advance for us to do."
—Ephesians 2:10 (NIV)

*In Week 1 of our study on a life in grace, we learned the foundational truth that "Improving your behavior will not give you victory in the Christian life." [2] We must all come to that point in our lives where we believe and trust in Christ for our only true identity.*

*We have to recognize the lies of the stolen identities we have all picked up and put on along this road of life. They may have been molded in our childhoods or sown by others into each of us through their sins. They*

---

[2]  Steve McVey, The Grace Walk Experience (Eugene, Oregon: Harvest House Publishers, 2005) p. 5

*may have been what we have placed upon ourselves from the things we have done and experienced through the lures of this fallen world. Or they are the lies the Enemy places on each and every one of us every day in an attempt to deceive, kill, destroy and steal the truth from us. Satan has given us masks of false identities to wear. These masks bring guilt, shame, rejection, and self-condemnation. Only our Creator can free us from this bondage and the fleshly strongholds that steal the life and light given to us through the truth of God and our true identity in Christ Jesus. We must all rest in the truth and realize that we don't need fixing. We are products of the Cross, no longer products of our past. God perfects us in Christ in every way, a work in progress that has not yet been perfected; but we stand on the promise of God that He isn't finished with us yet and He will finish the good work He has begun in us.*

"...being confident of this, that he who began a good work in you will carry it on to completion until the day of Christ Jesus."
—Philippians 1:6 (NIV)

*In Week 2 we learned the foundational truth that "Problems in your life could be the best thing that could happen to you."* [3] *This is part of His refinement process. This is how our Abba Father rids us of the junk in the trunk, by peeling away layers of our false identities: self-sufficiency, self-reliance, and misunderstood purpose, value, and significance.*

*I picture people in the likeness of this herd of strong-willed, out-of-control, wild stallions who are in complete rebellion, fully prideful, independent, and useless to their*

---

[3] McVey, p. 35

Master. We can't be used until we have been broken and have fully surrendered ourselves. We must be completely exhausted of the self-life in exchange for the Christ-life. The offer is to exchange the counterfeit for our Creator's original intent—to be partakers of Him. I can't think of a better way to break us and bring us to the end of ourselves than to allow trials, tribulation, turbulence, and impossible circumstances into our lives. Let's face it: we are hard-headed, strong-minded men and the word surrender is not in most of our vocabularies. James tells us, "Count it all joy when you fall into various trials." James 1:2 (NKJV)

Count it all joy? Whew!

In Week 3 we learned the foundational truth that "You must know who you are to change what you do." [4] This was one of the most difficult truths to get my heart wrapped around.

What we do and have done does not determine who we are. Knowing who we are in Christ determines what we do. This certainly goes against what the world teaches us today. In the seen realm, it is all about performance. As long as you can perform well enough, and long enough, the world will embrace and accept you.

In the kingdom and the unseen realm to which we now belong, performance is foreign and not recognized. In this realm, we are unconditionally accepted for who we are in Christ. It is so important to understand that we were made saints at the cross. We are holy, blameless, worthy and completely righteous in Christ. It is critical for us to recognize the truth that our righteousness is not achieved by us, but received by believing God's truths through faith in His grace.

[4] McVey, p. 67

*Receiving our identity simply comes from trusting and resting in who Christ says we are. Achieving our identity is simply performance-based and choosing to believe a lie about ourselves! The Christian life is not a changed life; it is an exchanged life, lived out of the truth and resources of the Father.*

*I want to share with each of you the struggles of a twenty-eight-year-old man who lives in a 10 foot by 10 foot prison cell at the Cinnamon Correctional Facility in Pushing, Oklahoma. He is serving out a 20 year sentence. His struggles are those of a simple-minded man who is new in Christ, walking through life without a clue of his true God- given identity. Sure, he reads his Bible daily. He has plenty of time to be in the Word.*

*He attends church three times a week and has a family who loves and misses him dearly. His primary focus each day is simply to survive while doing his best to improve his behavior, correcting himself in hope of an early release. He is trying to survive amongst the worst-of-the-worst criminal minds, gangs, murderers, rapists, and child-molesters. You name it, and he is smack dab in the middle of it.*

*This man is my son. Last Tuesday afternoon, he called from an illegal cellular phone to cry out for help. He called me in complete panic and pandemonium. He was trying to explain how much trouble he was in and that he had problems beyond anything I could comprehend. He was approached Monday morning in the yard by the Mexican Mafia, who offered him $500 to have his fiancée bring a package into the prison during visitation, which he agreed to do. He went on to describe a sting operation that took place outside the prison—where his fiancée was arrested and charged with drug trafficking and for bringing contraband into a state penal facility. This was a big problem.*

*He went on to explain to me that the Mexican Mafia told him that they didn't care about his fiancée. They wanted full payment for the drugs that had been seized. They gave my son a cell phone and told him to handle it. They wanted $1,000 or his life. My son has always been able to take care of himself; a bruiser, you might say, but this time things were beyond what he could bear or handle on his own.*

*The fact is, in prison things are radically different. There are two basic rules by which inmates live: if you snitch you will die; and, don't ever smuggle in contraband for an opposing ethnic race or gang. These are their laws.*

*Here lies one problem. My son has no money. If the Aryan Brotherhood catches wind of this activity or transaction, they would kill him. If he doesn't come up with the Mexican Mafia's money, they will kill him. My son was begging, crying, and pleading for me to go to Walmart and purchase a prepaid credit card and text him back with the cc code required to pay off these people. He needed this done immediately.*

*Initially, I agreed in haste and told him that I would do whatever he needed me to do—no questions asked! Once I got home from work, I was able to pray with my wife Bimini and wait on God for His guidance and direction. I waited an entire hour before racing out for Walmart, sick to my stomach and without a word from Holy Spirit. I knew that I was on my own, operating independently of the voice of God.*

*I sat in the parking lot of Walmart for more than two hours. I called my brothers in Christ, seeking wise counsel. I called my pastor and I literally began to pray without ceasing. I was being bombarded with in-bound text messages. These messages were now coming from a Mafia member, explaining that they now owned my son* and that they would kill him if either of us snitched. He also said that if I wanted my son back, I needed to send the money. I sat there like a deer in headlights.

I saw no route of escape for my son and I was faced with the biggest decision ever in my walk with Christ. I could send the money to the Mexican Mafia and sow into the wickedness and evilness of the world, using the resources God has entrusted to me and possibly save my son's life, or I could not send the money and trust God that He could and would deliver my son from this horrible situation.

My spirit was screaming out to me to walk away. This action would result only in compromising my walk and union with Christ. The next voice I heard was the enemy telling me that "It could all be over if I would just walk in and purchase the credit card and send the code to these people." Good vs. evil, light vs. darkness. Sowing into the spirit vs. sowing into the flesh. My son lives or my son dies. These were my thoughts. This was a spiritual battle like no other, taking place in my mind—tugging and luring my heart and soul to do wrong.

God was faithful. As I prayed, He spoke to me as clearly as a mid summer day, saying: "Tony, do you trust me? Do you really trust me with your life? Do you trust me now with your son's life? Don't you remember my child Daniel and those hungry lions? Don't you remember Abraham and his son Isaac? Trust me and rest in who I say you are. You can't fix this, but I can!"

God had given me clear direction and understanding of His way and I let my son know that I was not going to be able to help him with the money. It was the most difficult decision I've ever had to make; but God gave me peace that He would use this for my son's good and His Son's glory. Obviously, my son felt both betrayed *and abandoned by his father, which broke my heart. I explained to him that in this world mankind will always let him down, but Christ the Savior would always be there for him, never letting him down. I helped him understand that he didn't need me—he needed God, he needed life. This life can flow only from the Father to His Son and into His sons and daughters here on earth. This is the flow of the Divine Vine for which we were created: the poured-out life from within an abiding vessel at rest.*

*This was my Abraham-Isaac experience. I, too, left my only begotten son on the altar, leaving all the consequences to our all-loving Father for His favorable outcome, knowing that our Father in Heaven was completely faithful to provide my son with all he needed.*

*In all this, we can see the reality of the richness of a Father-saving-Son relationship. How precious, priceless, and beyond comprehension it is. A child has ultimate value, complete significance and acceptance in his Father's heart, so much that the Father would lay His very life down for His own children. We are His workmanship, His written poem, His priceless pearls, His always-being-loved children — we are His alone.*

*For all you men out there who have sons and daughters, love them with all your heart and know that God loves them much more. For all of us who are sons, know that our Father's love is perfect, unconditional, unfailing, and everlasting, regardless of how our earthly fathers may have failed us, abandoned us, or never knew us. The truth is, all of God's children were born into this world lost prodigals. Whether they realize it or want to admit it, it doesn't change the truth.*

*Christ loves you and so do I,*
*Big T*

CHAPTER 8

# The Epistle of a Son's Brokenness Leading to God's Wholeness

My beautiful band of brothers had been praying for and walking with me through my Abraham-Isaac moment. I invited them to celebrate the victory of Christ in our lives and a testament that God doesn't waste anything in our lives, but even uses evil for His good and glory.

> "Good Morning, Wildmen Brothers:
>
> I have really felt encouraged by the Holy Spirit and several of my brothers to share with you the good news regarding my son, Zack. It is the next chapter to the journey I shared with most of you back in June/ July (Abraham-Isaac moment). Mostly, I enjoy sharing the glory and love of our Heavenly Father and the testimonies with which He blesses us all, even in the midst of tragedy and what we sometimes see as hopeless situations in our lives.
>
> I am writing you all this morning to witness that in every situation and every storm of life, there is hope— the hope we have in our loving Savior, Jesus Christ!
>
> After the night I spent in the Walmart parking lot, I received a text from my dear friend and brother-in-Christ, Pastor Dave. It said, "I know things hurt but go

*home and draw close to Bimini and allow yourself to be ministered to by your wife." Oh, how it has become more of a reality for me that we need each other. As believers, our hearts are being knitted together. We were created for one another. Pastor Dave allowed the Spirit of God to give me those words and lead me back to my Eve— my precious wife, Bimini. As I walked in the door that night, Bimini was life and light to me. She was beaming with excitement to share a spoken Word from God that brought both of us into the joyful arms of Christ. We had peace in this impossible situation.*

*Since that night, weeks passed with no word from Zack. I had made exhaustive calls to the prison in my effort to know if Zack was still alive. It was the not knowing that made it so difficult, and with every call, the Holy Spirit was so faithful to bring me back to that River of Life (Zoe) described in John 7:38.*

*Upon returning from our family summer trip, I rushed to the mailbox and there it was: God's goodness—a letter in Zack's handwriting. It was one among many of the most precious gifts I had been given in my life.*

*These are the words of my beautiful son, Zackery:*

Dear Dad,

I thought you should know that I took care of my problem with them dudes. I sold my shoes, boots, radio, hot pot, fan, television, watch, chain, cross, all my shorts, and sweat pants. This got it all taken care of with the help of all I own and the $150 that you and Bimini had put on my books last month.

You'll never have to worry about that again — I swear on my life I'm done with all evil. I cried and prayed hard to Jesus, Dad, and I fill a whole new pair of shoes now. I know that nothing can hurt me if I don't give anything a reason to. I am so ashamed of what I got myself into and at the same time, I'm glad I did it because it took something that severe to realize what my life had become—nothing.

One good thing, Dad, I didn't have to sell my Bible and that seems to be all I ever really needed, that and your help in studying and learning all you have about Jesus. You are so strong in your walk with Christ and I want to feel like you too—untouchable with Christ on my side. Please write me back and enclose a study with questions and answers that will help to make me be as strong as you are in Christ. I will be patiently waiting for a response.

Love Always, Your Son,

Zackery

*As I have been writing Zack the last week or so, a little each day as the Lord has led me, I have realized how God has allowed so many to be touched, encouraged, and ministered to through Zack's testimony. He doesn't even know how his story is being used by our Almighty Father in Heaven and that he even has a testimony from God.*

*I am excited to share and encourage Zack in this morning's writing. I have been asked to speak to several groups here in Bradenton/Sarasota to share his story. Yesterday, a brother contacted me to come out to his company and to share God's testimony of Zack's life with over seventy of his employees, many of whom are women who have children who are or have been in jail or prison. It was simply the most amazing thing I ever saw. Who but God would have known all that comes through simple obedience and sharing the word of our testimonies?*

*I will leave you with a thought: consider how beautiful, wonderful and powerful our Heavenly Father can be in and through each of us when we just rest in Him and allow Him to use our every impossible life situation for His glory, praise and honor. Here is a young man, living in a 10 foot x 10 foot prison cell somewhere in Oklahoma; who is touching hurting men, women, and parents in crisis right here in Manatee and Sarasota Counties and doesn't even realize it. We have to share the testimonies that God has given us. We need to remove the masks we put on to cover up and hide because we are afraid of what people may think about us. Our Spirits hunger to come out and play with one another, to be built up by one another, and to allow our Father to bring us into the reality that love does not fail and there is no shame, guilt or condemnation for those of us who are in Christ Jesus.*

*Christ loves you and so do I,*

*Big T*

# CHAPTER 9

## The Epistle of Putting up the Glass Between a Father and Son

"Good Morning, Zack:

Well, we're finally back from our family mission trip, and what a wonderful trip it has been! It did my heart good to see you, Son. You have no idea how you have been missed by your family and how your sisters really enjoyed meeting their big brother for the first time that they can remember. What a lasting impact it has had on them.

We were able to spend time and share the love of Jesus with Bimini's Uncle Bill, your Uncle Mark and his girlfriend, Bimini's sister Tabby and her family, Bimini's friend Denise in Kentucky (whom you know). We were also able to make it out to see your grandma and grandpa, Uncle Patrick and Amanda, Kelly and Ralph, Wally and John, Kimmy and Mike and family, Aunt Jackie, Sheri, and so many others along this God-breathed journey.

We traveled through sixteen states and drove over 6,000 miles. We did all of this over six weeks and experienced some amazing God moments together as a family in Christ, leaving the life of Jesus on each and every one we encountered along the way—a normal Christian lifestyle.

Son, our time at the prison was one of the greatest highlights of our trip. It is a time we will not soon forget. If I can be honest with you, we were quite disappointed that we were robbed of our special visitation and full day with you. However, we were so very grateful and thankful when the warden called and said that he would allow us to have that precious hour with you behind the glass. The time we shared together as a complete family will be one of the greatest memories God has allowed me to experience on this walk with Him.

Although we consider ourselves blessed for all God allowed us to experience on this glorious day, we need to talk about it and I need you to understand what robbed us of a full family special visitation. Otherwise, I would not be a good father to you or a good steward and ambassador for Christ and all that He has entrusted me stewardship over—which includes you—He has given me stewardship over you, Son.

To be the father He desires and has called me to be, we have to address your behavior. Although what you do does not determine who you are, your genuine beliefs will determine your actions. This is what concerns me, because they are not in alignment with one another. Actions and behavior reveal. They do not define. Belief and reliance define.

Let me start by helping you understand that Zackery is not a product of his past or of the poor behavior he has been exhibiting

> *Actions and behavior reveal. They do not define! Belief and reliance define!*

lately. You are a product of the Cross, Son. Your behavior does not determine who you are. Only Christ does. As believers of the truth of God, we have been invited into an inheritance to partake of a divine nature, a newness of life — His life. He says we are righteous, holy, and have been set-apart for Him (sanctified). To be sanctified is a very cool process we all experience as Christians, to the degree we let God have His way as our life. It is the process of removing something or someone from ordinary use, and setting it or them apart for a very specific purpose or extraordinary use. For Christians, sanctification is the process of being moved from something and set apart for someone. We've been made new in Christ. For just believing and trusting what has taken place on our behalf, we have been moved from death into life. We are reborn as new creations in Jesus—fused together as one Spirit with Him. Yes, Christ is in you even on your worst day, with the very worst being known about you, regardless of what your feeler or thinker may be telling you about yourself.

Please read and reflect on the following Scriptures and ask the Holy Spirit to reveal the truth to you about yourself and Christ living in Zack. These verses of truth will reveal your true identity in Christ.

Son, it is critical that you know the truth about yourself—not what you believe to be true about Zackery, but the truth that will set you free (John 8:32). It is the truth about how your Heavenly Father sees you and what He has done for you, in order that you can begin to walk in the newness of reality about the new you. We have been clearly instructed to put off the old self and to put on the new self by our brother, the Apostle Paul. Forget about the old way of living, by trying to get your needs met apart from Christ. It just can't happen. It's impossible.

| TRUTH TO PONDER |
| :---: |
| Romans 3:22-36 |
| Romans 6:19-23 |
| Romans 12:1-2 |
| John 3:16 |
| John 10:10 |
| Galatians 2:20 |
| 2 Corinthians 5:17 |
| Colossians 1:26-27 |
| Colossians 2:6-15 |
| Colossians 3:1-17 |
| Colossians 3:20-25 |
| Colossians 5:13-14 |
| 1 John 2:15-16 |

"I am the vine; you are the branches. If you remain in me and I in you, you will bear much fruit; apart from me you can do nothing."
—John 15:5 (NIV)

"Jesus answered, 'For I am the way, the truth, and the life.
No one comes to the Father except through me.'"
—John 14:6 (NIV)

He is the only way. A life walked apart from Him is not life at all. It is not His way. It is walking with the Enemy and his ways are

the ways of the world which lead to death, darkness, and destruction.
—Romans 6:16; 2 Corinthians 7:20; 1 John 5:1-21

I want to tell you about what God revealed to me about our visitation, the truth about our day, and the things that led up to this day.

You see Son, God had blessed your mother and I with one beautiful son and we named you Zackery. God gave me authority and stewardship over you, just like any other father/son relationship in existence. Your mother and I didn't do what we were called to do under God's ultimate and divine plan and instruction, the ruling authority over every parent/child relationship. Instead, we were given the freedom to choose our ways. Your mom and I both made poor, selfish, and foolish choices along this journey called life.

These choices were tied to both natural and spiritual consequences. These consequences reaped separation and a downward spiral in all our relationships and in our thinking, which was canopied with darkness and lifelessness.

Our relationship started as separated from God as any could. It was based on sexual immorality and the lustful and perverted independent pleasures of the world, living together outside the marriage covenant of God. We cheated and lusted after other people even after we had taken each other's hand in marriage and entered into covenant. We could never receive God's blessing over our marriage, not because God didn't want to bless it, but because we were choosing against Him and therefore rejecting His blessing. Eventually, our marriage deteriorated into divorce. This is the means to an end and the scheme of the Enemy against all marriages, all relationships of all creation—apartness and eternal separation from God!

We were lost, blinded, lured, and carried away by the world and its possessions. There is always a price to be paid when we choose to separate ourselves from our Creator through an independent, rebellious, self-seeking lifestyle which is ruled and rooted in Adam (sin— the independent self-life).

There is no life in the Tree of the Knowledge of Good and Evil (in-Adam tree), regardless of the branch from which we choose to swing—good or evil. We were never created to eat from this tree of legalism and rules we could never keep. We were not created to only know about God. Instead, we were created for intimacy and to know Him on the deepest level—heart-to-heart. We were created by Him and for Him. It's one thing to know all about the contents of a bottle of water and how it was bottled and what spring it originated from. It's an entirely different experience to know what it tastes like to consume it fully as you actually become one with it, allowing it to satisfy, and quench your thirst.

You see, God has always had a perfect plan for each one of us. His desire is always to give us life full of oneness, a richness which includes the keys to His Kingdom, and a standard of eternal life that goes far beyond the seen and temporary realm in which we live. Our Father God in Heaven would have much rather seen me and your mom choose Him and respond to the invitation of a life hidden in Jesus, then becoming captivated and lured away into bondage by the shiny ojects of this world and the devices it uses to allow us to escape into a false reality.

He would have delighted in my submitting to Him and surrendering myself—allowing the Holy Spirit to guide me around the worldly obstacles to His loving grace. He would have rejoiced if I had made the choice to rear you in a Christian home and if I had trained you up according to His truth—that you would have been filled and influenced with biblical morals, raised up in Christ-likeness with a tamed heart and passion for loving Him and loving others as yourself. It didn't happen this way for you or for me, Son; but that's okay. His plan for us is absolute and therefore still in place and available to us today—it's not too late. Unlike us, He never chooses against us—we choose against Him. Unlike us, He never changes—He is the same today as He was in

> *Remember, we are not products of our past, but products of the Cross! We are forgiven, redeemed, resurrected, and always-being-loved children of the Cross.*

the Garden 2,000+ years ago, as He will be when He comes back to pick up His bride for a wedding date.

Scripture is quite clear that God's greatest desire was that I would have trained you up in the way you should go, so that when you got older, you would not depart from it (Proverbs 22:6). Your mother and I failed you as parents, but this is behind us and a part of the past. Remember, we are not products of our past but products of the Cross! We are forgiven, redeemed, resurrected, and always-being-loved children of the Cross. We are refugees who came home to the open arms of our all-loving Father.

Therefore, my initial "training you up" was less than desirable, but I still have been trusted with complete authority and responsibility of sowing the love and truth of Jesus Christ into your grown-up heart. This isn't from a position of having to because of God's moral law and commandments. It's for a much better reason—a reason much greater in comparison. It's because Tony in Jesus, a new, born again creation, desires to, because I love you and get to—all because of the Father's unconceivable and amazing grace.

Let's take a second to talk about the eternal, time-tested law of reaping and sowing and the consequences always associated with sowing into the fallen realm versus sowing into the Kingdom realm. Believe me when I tell you that this "law" is every bit as real as the law of aerodynamics or gravity. It is really black or white and simple enough that a child could understand it.

| | | |
|---|---|---|
| **Good** vs. Evil | **Spirit** vs. Flesh | **Righteousness** vs. Sinfulness |
| **Light** vs. Darkness | **Oneness** vs. Separation | **Kingdom** vs. World |
| **Truth** vs. Lies | **Joy** vs. Sorrow | **Kindness** vs. Cruelty |
| **Life** vs. Death | **Peace** vs. War | **Gentleness** vs. Harshness |
| **Love** vs. Fear | **Calmness** vs. Anxiousness | **Resting** vs. Resisting |
| **Order** vs. Confusion | **Humility** vs. Pride | **Receiving** vs. Rejecting |

You can see all that is good, right, and just is opposed by the things that result from a fallen and blinded world—things that are a result of rebellion, independence, bondage, and captivity.

First, you see the things found in Kingdom-minded thinking. You also see the fruit that is a result of our resting and abiding in the truth—the Risen Savior, Jesus Christ.

Secondly, you see things found in Worldly-minded thinking. You also see the fruit that is a result of our resisting and rejecting the Life for which we were all created. We were created by love for love Himself. Take time to read and reflect on John 15:1-17 and Galatians 5:16-26.

You should be able to clearly see, in everything we do moment-by-moment, we have been given a choice on how we will respond to life as He comes at us. We have been given a choice of what and to whom we will sow and reap. We choose the things of the King and Kingdom of God of Heaven or of the fallen kingdom (the world) under the temporary rule of Satan.

As we spend time seeking the face of Jesus our Lord, we are invited into and given such a clear understanding and ability to see the unseen things of a life in Christ. Then we begin to realize all we have been given in this inheritance and adoption, if we would just receive it: things such as His simple instruction on how to experience life, the realities from where life flows, and what life was always created to be. It's really quite intoxicating as it begins to consume you from the inside out.

Again, this is as you believe it, receive it and walk out of it! You rely upon His strength and divine influence over your heart, instead of relying upon your own effort and resting in rational and logical thinking. Our God is a super-rational and super-logical God, whose ways are far above our ways, but He has invited you in to partake in all of it.

As we choose to receive Him and respond from Him, He is faithful through the Holy Spirit living in us to instruct, teach, and guide us in how to walk out of the realities of life in a fallen world, by walking step-in-step with the light of truth. (Galatians 5:25; Galatians 5:16)

In 1 John 1:7, it says to walk in the light, for He is in the light. As we do this, we have fellowship with Him, honor Him, and we begin to be led into all truth. As a result, we reap Kingdom treasures. The same could be said about sowing into and reaping from the world. When we do this, we receive the things of the world, which all seem to lead us away from life and usher us into death and darkness. Please read and reflect on 1 John 1:5-10; Galatians 5:17-24.

It's quite simple, Son. If we were to sow apple seeds we'd reap apples. Corn seeds produce corn. As we choose to sow into the things of the world, we are assured to reap the evilness, brokenness and separation of the world—typically more than we sow and for longer than we sow.

With all that said, please understand another Kingdom principle: sin brings separation from God. That's because it's simply choosing independence of self over dependence on God. It doesn't necessarily sever an already-existing relationship with Him, but it certainly stalls and severs our fellowship with Him. The "I" is what separates. It stands for "independent" of God and means "to miss the mark" or "to not have a share in"—a share in the Life of Christ. Basically, anything that we choose to do to get our needs met apart from God is sin. You can count on separating yourself from Him.

It's an inwardly rebellious response towards Him—saying, "I choose not to trust you, but I choose to trust in myself or to trust in the mighty "I". The "I" of independence was the lie which led to the fall of mankind and is obviously rooted in pridefullness and rebellion. This was the deception of Satan in the Garden of Eden (Genesis 3:5): that we could be our own gods apart from the Creator Himself. So the counterfeiter manufactured his first lie to mankind, and this deception sent a wake of destruction through all time and space, separating mankind from its Creator.

Adam and Eve took the bait of the three-fold lie from the pit of hell. Part of the lie was dressed up as a half-truth, to get their eyes off God and His abundance to focus on themselves: what they didn't and couldn't have. The second part was hidden deeply below the surface of the first. Satan lured and deceived and then he spent a lifetime accusing, condemning, shaming, blaming, and tormenting the first marriage that ever came into existence, one which God made without spot or blemish; all rooted in love everlasting.

First, Satan implied that God never said that they were not allowed to eat of any tree in the garden. Eve was already on Satan's hook, as her eyes and attention were now fixed on what she knew she shouldn't have. She began to justify and buy into the trickery she was being fed, that God had somehow been holding back His best from both her and Adam. Responding to Satan she said, "We may eat of the fruit of the trees in the garden, but God said, 'You shall not eat of the fruit of the tree that is in the midst of the garden, neither shall you touch it, lest you die.'" (Genesis 3:2-3)

In the second part of his lie, Satan further enticed Eve with a shadow of doubt as he began the assault for her mind, contradicting what God had clearly said! Satan replied, "You will not surely die. For God knows that when you eat of it your eyes will be open ..." [to death, darkness, destruction through a natural fallen filtered lens, robbing you of your super-natural spiritual sight]. He went on with the third part: " ...and you will be like God," [equal with Deity] "knowing good and evil." Ask yourself this question: could Adam and Eve be any more like God at this juncture? No. God clearly tells us that He had created them in His image and likeness. (Genesis 2) Adam and Eve had already been given dominion over the earth and all creation as they began speaking out the identity, purpose and destiny of every living and created form of life on the planet. They walked daily with the Master Creator of the universe—a pretty good gig.

So the underlying lie of Satan that caused the fall of the world is: *You can be your own god!* The lie of the mighty "I" and the "self-life" entered the world as mankind handed over to Lucifer himself the keys to the Kingdom, their birthright and therefore their identity and inheritance. They swallowed the lie which empowered the Liar. All mankind inherited the curse of the fall of mankind, as we all came from the fallen seed of Adam—all except the Last Adam, Jesus

Christ, who was born of a virgin from the seed of the Holy Spirit, who overshadowed the chosen mother, Mary, in order to fulfill prophecy.

My point in all this is: we are always choosing in every moment of every day. Life is flooded with choices, which are all tied to either the Eternal Kingdom and a life abundant in Christ -or- they are tied to the temporary, perishing world and a life non-existent *in Adam*, which is covered by darkness with no hope and no future. Our choices are tied to *life* or *death*; *light* or *darkness*; *truth* or *lies*. We're either living or we're dying, there's no middle ground. It is so simple, but we get deceived along our way through the irrational and illogical thoughts within the mind. When we trust in the self-life and make wrong decisions along this journey—choosing the more popular route, the easier and wider road, and the luring ways of the world, there will always be a natural and spiritual consequence tied to our choice. The consequences of ungodly choices produce dead fruit and will always lead to our demise. They will also separate us farther from God. These are not punishments from God for our bad behavior, but the fruit produced as a result from living a life outside of union with Him by our own choosing. We choose separation by rejecting the hand of God.

When we believe, trust, and rely upon God and choose to make God-guided decisions on this journey—choosing the less popular route, the more difficult, narrower road, and the less attractive way, we will reap a consequence as well. These consequences of godly choices produce good fruit and always lead to life eternal, drawing us deeper into union with God. This life is in the Son. These are not rewards from God for good behavior, but the fruit produced as a result from living a life in union and oneness with Him as He originally intended. From which tree were we created to partake? Read and reflect on 1 John 2:15-17; Matthew 7:12-14.

Now, take time to give all this some thought and look back upon the simple choices you have made in life, Son. Start with Nada or before, if you wish. Allow your mind to come all the way to the present time. Ask yourself what type of seeds have you sown and what is it that you have reaped in return? Talk to God about your feelings. It's important to share your heart with Him, no matter what. He already knows your heart. He gave it to you when He was breathing you into existence, before the foundation of the earth, when He knitted you together in your mama's womb. Read and reflect on Ephesians 1:4; Jeremiah 1:5; 1 Peter 1:20; Psalm 139:13-14.

Now, can't you clearly see how this eternal God-given principle rules in our choices? Due to the poor choices you made in Nada— which God allowed, (as everything gets filtered through Him perfectly, sovereignly, and divinely), He has given the D.O.C. of the State of Oklahoma authority over you, in order to help shape your heart. He did it to offer you correction and refinement out of His glorious love for you, hoping that you will receive it and begin to trust His ways and plans for your life in Christ. He is doing just as any good father would do for a son whom he loves, but He is doing it on a Father-God level.

The Kingdom is all about order, because God is all about order. When we rebel against order and authority, we are rejecting God's hand and His Divine authority over us. We're choosing to sow into the antichrist and the darkened world, which is in direct conflict against God its Creator. Ultimately, we are bringing onto ourselves consequences that can result only in death and destruction—robbing us of Life. At this point, we become blinded, bound and separated from an all-loving Father who desires for us to have a change of mind and heart (repentance). He desires for us to submit, surrender and come back into a right relationship of thinking and choosing by following His ways and His beautiful, flawless plans for our lives.

Zack, every time you make the choice to pick up a cellular phone or post something to Facebook, you are choosing freely with a disobedient and rebellious heart to rest in Adam in the Tree of the Knowledge of Good and Evil; therefore putting glass up between you and God. You're choosing to rebuke the authority God has allowed to rule over you until you can learn to make better choices.

Again, the consequence for sin (anything you do independent

of God to get your needs met) is separation from God and we rob ourselves of the beautiful union oneness of fellowship and intimacy with Him. We rob ourselves of the abundant goodness He has planned and prepared for each of us in advance—abundance which He desires to pour out upon you and me so that we can begin to experience it fully, and more importantly, that we would experience the fullness of Him. Please read and reflect on Ephesians 2:10; John 10:10.

As you sat there with that thick, cold glass cast down between us, my heart hurt for you. I saw so clearly this sowing and reaping principle. The eternal law of the Kingdom and the consequences that separated a precious son from his loving father, who would lay down his very life for his boy.

As a father and a born again believer in Christ, I still have the freedom to choose to sow the seeds of sin (separation) and isolate myself from my Heavenly Father. But my choice is to consciously strive to rest in His goodness moment-by-moment, choice-by-choice; to acknowledge His presence and abide in His warm embrace—allowing Him to guide me to the way, the truth, and the life He has prepared for me! Please read and reflect on Hebrews 12:2; Galatians 5:13; John 14:6.

Son, please choose to trust God by inviting and receiving Him into every circumstance, every choice around every hidden corner of your life and He will be faithful to deliver you from the power, delusion and deception of darkness. He is faithful to lead you into all truth and to help you right your thinking in relation to the Kingdom of Christ where you rightly belong as His adopted and redeemed always-being-loved child. Please read and reflect on Colossians 1:13; John 16:13; Romans 8:15-17.

Please consider the beautiful choice you have in Jesus. It is the only way to the life you have been promised. Don't let Satan continue to kill, steal and destroy the truth of the mystery hidden for ages and the hope of Glory—Christ Jesus in Zack. Please read and reflect on Colossians 1:13-14; 1 John 5:1-21; Colossians 1:27.

With Eternal Love & Blessing,
Dad XOXO
PS: If you can glean one thing from all of this, let it be this—
God's grace! Son, grace is simply this: That your Daddy in Heaven
loves you in such a way that He
could never love you any more
than He does on your worst day
with the very worst about you fully

> *The grace of God that is always greater than our sin!*

known to Him. Regardless of what you have done, what you are
doing, or what you will ever do, He can never love you any less. Please
read and reflect on 1 Corinthians 1:4; Ephesians 2:8-9.

# CHAPTER 10

## The Epistle of Love & Truth for a Son

Good Morning, Son:

I can't begin to tell you what a joy it brought to my heart to receive your letter yesterday. I have been waiting eagerly to hear from you, Son. Let me explain that many months ago the Lord had spoken to my heart about a couple of things while you were experiencing the many consequences of your choosing—lockdown, privileges being taken away, the fights and getting beaten; having your jaw broken. It was so much for a father to bear and I felt that my hands were tied, but I wanted to help you desperately. I wanted to rescue you from all the moments of pain and suffering you had to endure.

God had spoken clearly to me, that I couldn't save you, and that He is the only One that can rescue us from our self-life. He had begun that process in you son the day I held you in my arms in that county jail cell in Nada, Oklahoma where we prayed and cried out to God together. What a glorious day He gave us both. This was the day that God had made. It was the day He heard the voice within the depths of your heart, Son. As we prayed for your salvation, He opened the windows of Heaven and planted the seed of His life into the innermost part of your heart. He began pouring into you everything He had accomplished for you on the cross—abundant life. This all remains true, regardless of how much of it He has made you or me aware. Truth is truth.

During this time, God spoke to my heart about not being able to save you; He also spoke to me about you needing time in the wilderness, a season of time to realize the reality (what God sees) of where and from whom life originates and how your behavior was in complete misalignment with the truth about Zack. You need to know that our behavior can never define who we are. Only God can enlighten and awaken us to this reality. Holy Spirit said clearly that my preaching and teaching and leading and loving were falling upon deaf ears and a hardened heart; that you were not ready to hear the things that I was trying to teach and show you about your true identity in Jesus Christ.

This was the reason for my silence, Son. It was not because of the lies with which Satan has tried to deceive you—those whispering voices of condemnation, guilt, shame and rejection. The spirit of abandonment that's telling you that your dad doesn't love you because you're not lovable due to the things you have done. That condemning chatterbox telling you that your family has abandoned you and therefore we are somehow ashamed of you because of who you have become. The accuser trying to convince you that you have nobody but your useless self and you are somehow a disappointment and embarrassment to all those on the outside of those prison walls. The voice that comes like a roaring lion trying to have you believe that you are a waste of oxygen and your life no longer matters—that you are out of sight and therefore out of mind, and everybody you care about in this world has forgotten you. These are lies directly from the pit of hell—nothing could be further from the truth.

These are the things that are keeping you in bondage, Son, not those prison bars or barbed wire fences surrounding that lifeless yard. Let me tell you, Son, the Apostle Paul penned much of God's word of the New Testament from prison, yet Paul was as free as could be. His chains were broken on the road to Damascus (Acts 9).

This is the voice of the enemy, the spirit of the antichrist; and these are the deceptions that he uses to lure us away from God. Always drawing us into darkness in order to blind us and drag us deep into the pit of death and destruction. It is this deception that is actually blinding us from the love, light and life of Christ.

Satan was our greatest adversary. The good news is that Satan was defeated in every way, shape and form on the Cross of Calvary and He that lives in you is greater than he who doesn't live in you, but who lives and rules in the world and its fallen natural realm (1 John 4:4).

In John 10:10 (ESV), Jesus clearly reveals this truth to us. He says: "The enemy comes to kill, steal and destroy, but I came that you may have life and life to the full." In many translations it says, "have life abundantly."

> I like to think of it like this: if truth is what God says, then reality is what God sees.

Okay. With all that said you now can rest in the reality of truth that I love you without exception and nothing or nobody can ever take, change, steal, rob or alter my love for you, Son. My love is not contingent on your having it all together, your behavior, or your fixing yourself in any way. The same goes far beyond for God, so much more than we can understand or imagine. I can love you like this only because, just like Paul on the road to Damascus, I was once blind. Now I have been given sight to see that it is no longer I who live, and therefore it is no longer I who love, but Christ who now lives and loves in and through me (and you too). Again, reality and truth are synonymous to one another and interchangeable in the original Greek languge. I like to think of it like this: If truth is what God says, then reality is what God sees.

First let me tell you how proud I am of you and the goodness that you are pursuing in these classes about dealing with your anger issues, about *Sense of Self* and *Sense of Family* (not sure what N/A is, maybe *Narcotics Anonymous?*) and that you are now attending church. This is awesome news. It fills my heart with joy and happiness to know that there is a new fire and passion for living from Christ, burning deep within my beautiful boy Zack. I clearly see God working in and through His precious Zackery and now awakening you to the newness of life and the transformation that He is working out within you—it only keeps getting better, Son; better beyond comprehension, as He draws you into the depths of Himself, revealing layer after layer of His character and compassion for all humanity.

Please understand that God has given me, as dad, spiritual ears to hear my children, and so I am always listening to your heart in the things I hear you say in your letters and I will always see the goodness in your intentions and understanding. I have also been called to be a good father to you by bringing the rod of correction to your darkened understanding in love, so that you may know the truth of God; and therefore I will always come alongside you in order to help equip you with the purest filter for both your world and spiritual views. But ultimately, a clear lens through which to see can come only from the Spirit within you, the Holy Spirit Himself. Read and reflect on John 14:26; 1 Corinthians 6:19.

Please don't misconstrue the things I am going to share about what I have seen and heard in your letter. There is no negative in this; only a father who loves his son enough to bring him truth by lovingly coming alongside to edify and build him up in Christ; never with any intent to harm or tear down what God has so beautifully and wonderfully created. I want and need you to know that you are beautifully and wonderfully made. My precious Zackery, you are God's always-being-loved-child and we are all so thankful for you.

I heard the leading of the Lord say, " Go back and carefully listen to the words of Zack's heart. Help him by extracting the lies and implanting My truth. Let him know words are powerful—words create worlds."

The following is a letter broken down by a father who cares about what his son thinks of himself and those around him:

The "light that popped on in your head", is God and God alone, because He is the "way, the truth, the life and the light." Light can come only from its source—God. When we first believed, we were brought into the light, the light was brought into us and now we get to partake in being light to others around us ... This is the most beautiful part of our newness, our inheritance, and oneness with God.

Christ in you and you in Christ—you have been made new, not fixed or rebuilt, but made completely new. You see, Son, we were all so bad off, not even God could fix us. He had to crucify us with His

Son, Jesus. It was a co-crucifixion, as we had to die in order to be made alive—we had to die to self in order to be made alive in Christ. Paul tells us in Philippians 1:21 (ESV), *"For to me to live is Christ and to die is gain."* Please read and reflect on John 17; Matthew 5:14-16; 2 Corinthians 4:4; 2 Corinthians 5:17; Galatians 2:20. You will begin to see the pattern of truth to which God wants to reveal and awaken all creation—the crucifixion was a co-crucifixion and the answer to Jesus's prayer in the garden by His loving Father.

The "simple reality" of which you spoke is the simple truth into which God has been leading, guiding, and wooing you—this is His prevenient Grace. "The reality that you are alone in there" is certainly a reality. It's a false reality, or the opposing force to the truth: a lie from the liar.

The truth is you have never been alone for one moment in there. Christ has been in you all along, waiting for you to choose life over death, the light over the darkness, goodness over evil. Go back to the sowing and reaping letter I wrote and ask the Holy Spirit to reveal the truth about all those things I shared with you regarding our freedom to choose a lie over the truth, to choose death over life—it is no longer in our new nature to choose the old ways of thinking.

The simple truth is that in all of our moment-by-moment choosing we are given freedom by God to choose the Holy Spirit over the spirit of flesh, the Spirit of God over the spirit of the Antichrist, the truth over a lie, the light over the darkness, the way of the Kingdom over the ways of the world. It can never be both. It's one or it's the other. This is why Paul warned us to take every thought captive to the obedience of Christ and to set our minds on things above, not on the things below. To be transformed by the renewing of our minds and not conformed to worldly ways; to put off the old-self and to put on the new-self, to walk in the Spirit and not in flesh. Read and reflect on Colossians 3:2; 2 Corinthians 10:5; Romans 12:2; Ephesians 4:22; Galatians 5:25.

The part in your letter about "at the end of the day Jesus is watching over you" is absolute truth, Son, and exactly what I'm saying about resting in the unseen things. But see the lingering half-truth, which is nothing more than a lie that Satan would have you believe about your current circumstance: that you're alone; that you're out of sight and therefore out of the minds of those who love you most. These are two conflicting thoughts that you have to resolve, Son. Watch for the leaven that the enemy uses to taint the truth. It just takes one degree to pollute the truth of God. The enemy does not have to get us off by much (1 Corinthians 5:6-8).

You are either alone in there, or you have Jesus watching over you each and every moment of every day. Which is it? It can't be both. Can you see the deception and double-minded thinking that the enemy uses, the half-truth that he dresses up as a counterfeit? His design is to lure us into a false reality about ourselves, others, and our temporary circumstances, thereby blinding and binding us from the face of Jesus and His divine influence over our lives.

*Grace – God's divine influence over our hearts.*

If we are in Christ, we are no longer double-minded. Instead, we are Christ-minded—walking in faith together, hand-in-hand, living in union with Him in one Spirit and one Mind. Read and reflect on James 1:8; 1 Corinthians 2:16; Philippians 1:27.

Obviously the truth, is that nothing and nobody can ever separate you from Christ and His love for you, Son. Read and reflect on Romans 8:31-39—you are never alone anymore, Son.

"Pushing hard and trying to open the doors of that prison" is another trap and snare from the enemy (2 Timothy 2:26). Beware of trying instead of trusting. You can choose to trust God to get you out of prison by asking, seeking and knocking; in complete faith and confidence that He can, He will, and He wants to release you, Son. Or you can choose trying on your own strength, which always leads to a dead-ended path. John 15:5 tells us that apart from Him we can do nothing, but in and through Him, we can do all things (Philippians 4:13).

*You apart from Christ is simply a lie.*

Here is the difference between the two choices you face right now: one comes from God and one comes through the independent nature and a life lived apart from God; which, again, is a lie from the spirit of the antichrist. Here is a list of what is represented by the two trees that were in the Garden of Eden—the tree of the knowledge of good and evil and the tree of life (Genesis 2:7-9; 2:16-17). This is a foundational part of understanding God's intent for mankind and the relationship for which we were all created.

The tree of the knowledge of good & evil is what I call the *trying tree*. The tree of life is what I call the *trusting tree*. You must understand that you were naturally born into the independent flesh tree (the tree of knowledge of good and evil) but by God's divine design and original intent, you had to be born again into the tree for which you were created, the Christ-dependent spirit tree, the tree of grace (Genesis 2:9; John 3:3).

It is important to understand that the tree of knowledge of good and evil has two branches, the evil branch and the good branch. Every human being ever created was born into and began trying to live from the tree of the knowledge of good and evil and each of us swings from one or between both of these two branches; and so I also call it the in Adam tree. For forty-six years I swung between two branches of good and evil, completely blinded from the truth that there was actually another tree—the Tree of Life.

Don't get me wrong. God created both trees in the Garden and will forever protect the integrity of freedom of choice and the free will of mankind. So they are both good, as everything from God is good. But we all needed to experience the tree of death in order to come to the tree of life. I think every human being must taste what life isn't in order to get to what life is.

# The Tree of the Knowledge of Good and Evil vs. The Tree of Life

| THE TREE OF THE KNOWLEDGE OF GOOD AND EVIL | THE TREE OF LIFE | THE TREE OF THE KNOWLEDGE OF GOOD AND EVIL | THE TREE OF LIFE |
|---|---|---|---|
| Lying Tree | Truth Tree | Trying Tree | Trusting Tree |
| Temporal Tree | Eternal Tree | Flesh Tree | Spirit Tree |
| Entitlement Tree | Contentment Tree | Tree of Fear | Tree of Faith |
| Guilty Tree | Innocent Tree | The "I" Tree | The "Thy" Tree |
| Defeated Tree | Victorious Tree | Self-Tree | Savior-Tree |
| Pride Tree | Humility Tree | Hating Tree | Loving Tree |
| Becoming Tree | Being Tree | Tree of Chaos | Tree of Order |
| Self-Dependent Tree | Christ-Dependent Tree | Tree of Separation | Tree of Union |
| Tree of Anxiousness | Tree of Peace | Ownership Tree | Stewardship Tree |
| Concealed Tree | Revealed Tree | In-Adam Tree | In-Christ Tree |
| Rejecting Tree | Receiving Tree | Conforming Tree | Transforming Tree |
| Tree of Good Intentions | Tree of Grace | Worldly Tree | Kingdom Tree |
| Striving Tree | Abiding Tree | Tree of Apartness | Tree of Oneness |
| Resisting Tree | Resting Tree | Dying Tree | Living Tree |
| Close-Fisted Tree | Open-Handed Tree | Tree of Darkness | Tree of Light |
| Law Tree | Grace Tree | Condemning Tree | Acquitting Tree |
| Tree of Antichrist | Tree of Christ | Sorrow Tree | Tree of Joy |
| Self-Centered Tree | Others-Centered Tree | Bondage Tree | Freedom Tree |

You get the point. We want to be sure that we are in the tree that is aligned with the truth about us and our God-given identity in Christ. Regardless of our feelings, poor behavior, and often condemning thoughts from the enemy, we have to set our minds on the truth that we have been made new in Christ (2 Corinthians 5:17) and that there is only one tree from which to partake. As Christians, we are products of the tree of life and are now dead as a bag of hammers to the tree of the knowledge of good and evil. We are forevermore products of the cross, never again products of our past (Galatians 2:20).

In his letter to the Philippians, Paul basically admitted that nobody swung higher, longer, and with more precision and accuracy than he did from the tree of the knowledge of good and evil, but now that he had been awakened to the tree of life, he counted whatever gain he once had as a complete loss.

Paul says in Philippians 3:8 (ESV), *"Indeed, I count everything as loss because of the surpassing worth of knowing Christ Jesus my Lord. For his sake I have suffered the loss of all things and count them as rubbish, in order that I may gain Christ and be found in him, not having a righteousness of my own that comes from the (the tree of knowledge of good and evil) law, but that which comes through faith in (tree of life) Christ, the righteousness from God that depends on faith—that I may know him and the power of his resurrection, and may share his sufferings, becoming like him in his death, that by any means possible I may attain the resurrection from the dead. Not that I have already obtained this, or am already perfect, but I press on to make it my own, because Christ Jesus has made me his own."*

Son, I read your words, "I even lost hope in myself and forgot that I am the king of my own temple. This ball is ultimately in my court. I had no goals; my morals had all been adjusted to fit in my environment, chameleon-like. Everything about me had changed from the first time I stepped in the D.O.C. But now I see plain as day that this is no place to want to fit into. I want now to stick out like a sore thumb. I try to lead by example now and anyone who follows on their own accord, I accept in my circle and try to teach them all I know about getting out of here alive and with self-set goals and even dreams to achieve."

You make mention several times throughout your letter about "being the king of my own temple". This would be a lie from the pit of hell and the spirit of the antichrist would love to use it to keep you self-focused, self-conscious, sin-conscious, and sense-conscious, in order to keep you thinking, feeling, and choosing independently from your Creator; and therefore separated and blinded from life itself.

John tells us this clearly—"This is the testimony, Father God has given us eternal life, this life is in the Son, he who has the Son has life, he who does not have the Son of God, does not have life." —1 John 5: 11-12 (ESV)

There is only one King. He is the King of Kings and His Name is Jesus (Timothy 6:15). Sure, because God is sovereign and just, He allows us the choice to be the king of our own temples and to swing freely from the tree of independence, which has no life and no lasting value of any kind. From it we can do nothing, as we were never created for it. As Christians, we actually died to it. —John 15:1-5 (ESV); Romans 6:1-14 (ESV)

The lie is separation. We were created for union and to walk in one Spirit. This is the void in every human's life which can't be filled with the things seen in the natural; it is the divine itch that can't be scratched with the things found in the world. The only thing that can satisfy and bring lasting relief is Christ alone. Christ plus nothing. Please get this, Son. We were created to love and to be loved by the lover and creator of all men. This isn't something you have to try harder to achieve, work longer to earn, do better to obtain—it doesn't come to us by striving, working, trying, doing, or becoming—it comes only by being, trusting, and receiving into what has already been accomplished for you through Jesus on the Cross. In His last utterances on the cross was **"Tetelesti."** This means simply, **"it is finished."** You are finished in Christ. You are completely loved, valued, and significant with a purpose beyond measure—now count it all to be true and begin walking out of it regardless if you fully understand it or not. God said it. Believe it.

You see, Son, you were bought with a price, and you are no longer your own. Our brother Paul said it so clearly and beautifully to the church in Corinth: [emphasis added] "Or do you not know" [Have you not heard the truth about the tree that was created and has always existed for you, the Tree of Life] "that your body is a temple of the Holy Spirit within you, whom you have from God? You are not your own, for you were bought with a price. So glorify God in your body (1 Corinthians 6:19-20).

Losing hope in ourselves is not necessarily a bad thing, Son. It was the best thing that had ever happened to your dad. I think that when I finally said that I can't live this life of trying to become what the world says I should be, that God smiled down upon me and said, "Thanks be to Me." Thank God. I realized the truth through my own hopelessness—the hopeless lies found in living from the tree of the knowledge of good and evil.

They are the lies of self-reliance, self-sufficiency, self-centeredness, self-entitlement, self-righteousness, self-sustaining, self-preservation, self-hope, self-everything. Haven't you noticed that we live in a world of "self-help". Self-help books, videos, infomercials—they are a snare from Satan himself. If we buy into the lie that we become through our doing, the world will embrace us only as long as we can perform for it. This rabbit hole leads us down two, dead-ended slippery slopes—he wears us out through performance-based acceptance or we believe that we're just not good enough to begin with. Either way it always ends in a life of trying harder to become acceptable—a lie within a lie.

We were not created for oneself. We were created for something far greater—we were created by God and for God; and now we live in God. Did you know that God has always been trying to get into you, so that He can get out of you what He has divinely placed within you—Christ. Christ wants to express Himself in and through you, Son (Galatians 2:20; 2 Corinthians 5:17; Romans 6:3-11). Hope in yourself—No. Hope in money—No. Hope in 401k retirement plans—No. Hope in the world or things found in this world—No. Instead, hope in what is within you—Christ and Christ alone (1 Timothy 6:17; 1 Peter 3:15).

Paul tells the church of Colossae about the hope of glory. In Colossians 1:26 (ESV) he says, "The mystery hidden for ages and generations but now revealed to his saints [you and I]. To them God chose to make known how great among the Gentiles [you and I] are the riches of the glory of this mystery, which is Christ in you, the hope of glory." The hope of glory is Christ living in you, Son.

So as a beacon of the light and life of Christ, you will *"stick out like a sore thumb"* in there, believe me. Think about how the Apostle Paul must have stood out as he touched people from around the world and within the Roman prison system, who were watching him rejoice in his sufferings. Read about Paul's sufferings. They are too extensive to imagine (2 Corinthians 11:16-30). Yet he was able to look beyond his circumstances to Christ in whom he was supernaturally able to live above all his problems, because he knew that it was no longer he who lived, but Christ in him. Paul realized that a life of 70-100 years here in the world was a lie from the ruler of the world, who comes dressed up as an angel of light. Paul was looking at the world through a Kingdom lens, not the temporal lens where "life ends in death." Paul says throughout New Testament Scripture that he was merely a stranger, passing through this worldly realm. Recently I had revelation regarding this kind of thinking and I posted it to Facebook:

> *"With all the abundance along every facet of this journey called living, I now find myself with a new life now completely secure, full and flowing over with the richness of knowing my identity as a newly created spiritual being who is traveling through this fallen world of hopelessness, darkness, and deterioration as a mere stranger passing through this seen and temporary realm. As I am carried onward towards eternity, I am awakened to and surrounded by these divine opportunities to love others well and share with them this exchanged, co-crucified life to which I am now pleasantly a prisoner, as a sort of bond-servant in-Jesus.*

*I think to myself, if living is Christ—then He is for me, dwelling within me and desiring to live His life through me. It's a Christ-life. And so then I realize I must fully surrender every thread of my being to the One who is love, life, and light to all the darkness that surrounds me in this seen and fallen season where I find myself.*

*And so now I can see clearly the truth that He wants to get into me so that He can get out of me in order to freely express Himself through me. Along this adventure called life, we all have to experience what life isn't in order to come to who, where, why, and what life is: Christ in me, a beacon of love to the world that knows no love. Heaven on earth? And to the degree you rest in Me, you will impart life to all those within our shadows."*

So when you begin to live *from* Christ instead of *for* Christ, your joy will become contagious and off the charts. People around you within those walls will want to follow Zack in Christ because they will see the hope of being set free from the self-life and the newness of walking as the spiritual beings they were created to be before the foundation of this planet we call earth (Ephesians 1:3-14). Christ-centeredness versus Self-centeredness. One leads to life. The other leads to death.

Okay, enough preaching, teaching, and leading—it's time to focus on the real reason I am writing you. When I woke up this morning, I just wanted to tell you how much I love you and miss you, son. How I often think of you each day and imagine you on the outside walking beside me as I show you these things I share with you in words, walked out in the everyday actions of a simple man in a fallen and complex world. Son, God created you ultimately for Himself, but always intended us to be together as father and son. Oh, how I miss your beautiful smile and that wonderful sense of humor that can light up any room.

I think about your innocence as a young child growing up; your shyness the first time I saw you get off that airplane in Denver. You were six years old and I saw myself in you in so many ways. I think about all the times we have shared in our former lives, and I thank God every day that I had those special times with you in all my blindness and lifelessness just the same. I remember traveling out to Uncle Patrick's wedding together and I treasure having that time with you, Son. It will be forever special to me. I hold our moments together in the depths of my heart.

I miss you so much and I want time with you so desperately, but ultimately the most important thing for me is that you experience the bondage-breaking freedom that Christ has allowed me to know and live today—it is exhilarating and beyond my simple words, Son. If I were in your shoes (and I wish I could take your place in prison), I would want to be living these truths out and experiencing what life was really always intended to be. I could be walking within those prison walls 18 inches off the ground for all to see and come to know the free gift of Jesus living His life in and through me. It is an exchanged life.

So as I close this letter that I have been co-writing you with our Daddy in Heaven, I want to leave you with some encouraging truths to consider for yourself with God. Please get with Abba Papa and search the Scriptures for yourself like a good Berean; but more importantly, have ears to hear what He wants to say to you personally, Son (Acts 17:11; Romans 10:17; John 5:39-40).

You are loved, accepted, significant, valued with great purpose, worthy, free, victoriously adored, defended, protected, accompanied, celebrated, admired, befriended, bought-and-paid-for, adopted, restored, renewed, remade, and reborn.

Son, our family misses you with our whole hearts and we are for you, praying with you, hoping just as the father of the prodigal son did, watching out these windows, and patiently waiting to see you come home. I would give anything to throw my arms around you and to kiss your neck, if only to feel the warmth of your embrace for a single moment, Son. I love you endlessly and God loves you more.

Standing with you,
Dad XOXO

# CHAPTER 11

# A Father Learning to Hear
# the Voice of the Father

It was early November, 2014, out on the dock in my backyard. I had been learning to hear God's voice through practicing something called "two-way journaling." It was through this precious and priceless quiet time that I experienced the divine calling of my Abba Papa, telling me *to go and feed His sheep.*

*Journal 11-11-2014 (On the Dock): "Tony, do you see us together resting in the big yellow inner-tube, floating with no particular direction or path except that of what is unseen as the wind gently blows us in this divine circle? This is what life is. It's resting and abiding in the preserver of life together, enjoying a life of grace. Can you feel My grace, Tony? Do you feel the freeness you have in Me? There are no cords binding us to land, yet there is perfect control regardless of the exterior winds blowing … I AM … The coolness is my comfort. Feel My coolness over your entire body and feel the warmth of My love shining down upon you from the sunshine I created and breathed out for you … This was created to engulf you with the serenity and security of My warmth when you allow Me to embrace you."*

"This reminds me of what the coolness of the garden must have been like, felt like, smelt like. I feel at perfect peace when I'm out here with You, Papa, when it's just the three of us together soaking up all

Your glorious creation with everything in Your strong and mighty hands.'

*"Tony, do you notice that there is no set course before you, but only a flow that I control as we float confidently along, full of life and love together. Feel My breath being breathed through your breathing, Son. Can you feel Me sustain you completely; fully in control but allowing you to manage the tempo and depth or shallowness of each breath? Tune out the cars and tune out the building that is going on around you. Yes, Tony, that was a huge fish. Now focus back on us. You never have to leave this place unless you choose to. I created it for you, precious boy! I delight in the having and holding one another and there is no place I'd rather be ... Most of My children don't spend this kind of time with Me. Sweetness of Life. I created you for it!"*

'What did you create me for, Papa?'

*"For Me and for your brothers and sisters. You have so many ... Help Me, son ... feed My sheep ... I adore you, Tony. In all your resistance, I love you. Learn to soar with Me in our walking together. Let Me teach you how to get out of the boat and walk with Me on the water of Life itself, as nothing is as it appears in your mind; I will help you get out of your mind. That's why we're here today, spending Sweetness together.*

*Just love Zackery every way imaginable. He needs only the love from his Father. Tell him how we spend time together. Teach him to hear My voice! He hears voices but often they're not Mine. I want to have and hold Zack like you do. Go feed my sheep. My plans for you are to spend an eternity of days and nights like this together—love you, Son ...Daddy"*

It was as clear as day to me that I needed to contact Zack. I wanted to be obedient and sat down and began to write. Again, I heard the voice deep within say, *"Don't write Zack another letter. He will interpret it as cold and lifeless. I said go and feed my sheep."*

It really doesn't get much clearer than that, so I began the process of searching what it would cost to fly out immediately to Oklahoma City, rent a car and stay for a couple days. As my wife Bimini researched this online, it looked like about $2,500 for the trip. My first thought was to look for something 2-3 weeks out and with some advance notice to bring the airfare down. As I began to negotiate with God, He simply asked me, "*My $2,500 or yours, Tony?*" Bimini booked everything as our family Priceline queen and the final price for the entire trip came in under $600. This was our first confirmation from God.

The second confirmation came after calling the prison to find out if I could even see Zack. I spoke with his unit manager and she told me that a special visitation usually takes 4-6 weeks to get approved. I explained that I had heard from God and knew that this was meant to be. I let her know that I had booked my flight already and would be arriving in Oklahoma City Thursday afternoon. She said she would call me some time Friday to let me know what she was able to do.

*Journal 11-13-2014 (Before the Flight):* A divine word to me from my dear and precious brother Pastor Bill Baker — "Taste Me".

*Journal 11-13-2014 (In flight):* I had been entrenched in *4 Keys to Hearing GOD's Voice (Virkler).* As I gazed out the window, I simply asked the Lord to reveal Himself to me. Within seconds, I saw clearly in the clouds the formation of Jesus's face, His eyes and nose, His mouth and lips and His glorious, infectious smile. As quickly as it appeared, it was gone. I thought to myself, "On the way back home, I'm definitely requesting a window seat!" I began to speak to God, saying: "Abba Papa, I want to know what it is to taste You, what it means to completely and fully savor Your Being upon my palate, oh Lord."

While pondering this thought, I was led to this beautiful invitation from God—"*Oh taste and see that the LORD is good! Blessed is the man who takes refuge in him*" Psalm 34:8 (ESV). This was my third confirmation that God was divinely present and guiding faithfully!

*Journal 11-15-2014 (Before Zack's visitation, prison parking lot prayer):* As I sit here with You, Papa, You have once again brought me into tears of joy as You placed in my heart the story of the Prodigal Son and the imagery of a brokenhearted father who ran from afar for his son, who had come home. As the father threw his loving arms around his son's neck, he hushed all the regret, the shame, the "I'm sorry's", and the "will you forgive me's."

I thought, "I am going to be able to run for my son this morning. A celebration is in order." In that moment, I knew it was time to lift our day up to the One who had made it all possible.

"I surrender all, Papa. I lay myself at the altar as a living sacrifice for You, that I could be used as a righteous vessel for Your glory and honor in this darkened place today; that You would rule and reign in this priceless time with Zack. Help me focus on Your love and light for both of us. Pour out of me the things You want to say and that You desire Zack to know and see into.

Father, I pray that not one word that proceeds out of my mouth be my own, but be of the One who sent me, the One who formed me, the One who made me new. I desire only to be Your truth-teller today and every day, with no agenda except Christ, crucified for all of us! Hold me, keep me, and protect my mind from the Enemy who will surely attempt to disrupt our day. Help me to see above his ploys and plundering of this divine time You have breathed out for Your child Zack. I pray that they would all see and hear Jesus as they watch a father run for his son, bathe him in truth, clothe him in his rightful robe given by You, with the ring of his true identity upon his finger and the truth of Sonship slipped upon his feet—not because either of us is worthy of anything, but because of the blood of the Lamb upon that magnificent cross and my Savior's body stripped for the healing of us all. Amen"

As I got through all the security, body searches, and cold metal doors, I could see Zack from across the room and just as Daddy had revealed to me, I ran across that visitation room and threw my arms around my son's neck, allowing him to pick me up into his arms as we just held each other and tried to take in all the sweetness God had allowed for us in the unforgettable moment—truly a glimpse into the joy of Heaven.

Once we were able to wipe away all the tears of joy, we sat down and Zack was immediately approached by an inmate who whispered something into his ear. Zack's attention turned to something across the visitation room. I had great discernment that the Enemy had come to begin to thwart the plans of God; that he had come to steal this precious time from us. I told Zack that I needed to know what was going on. He gave me a quick "nothing, Dad." His attention soon began to drift from our conversation again and I explained to him that if we didn't get out into the light whatever it was that was luring his mind and heart away from the things God wanted to say through me, God would not be able to defuse it. He never works out of the things hidden away in darkness but only out of what is brought into His marvelous light in loving truth.

After I pressed him, Zack spilled the beans and told me he was being solicited to bring back into the prison contraband that had made its way into the visitation room. If he did this, he would be forgiven debt that he had accumulated during some backsliding months prior. He was heartbroken about this as he wept like a baby. He confessed that the reason he resisted telling me was that he didn't want me to compromise my walk with God by sowing into such wickedness.

I explained what God had spoken clearly to me; that I was to love him every way imaginable and this was certainly something I would interpret as imaginable, but that I would never sow God's resources into anything like this again, ever. I told Zack to get up and go tell the Enemy's camp that the debt was paid in full.

Zack walked across the room and by the look on the face of the large, tattooed, and pierced man he had approached, he had shared the good news—paid in full. Then I was brought to tears as I watched Zack walk over to a nearby bookshelf, where he picked up two old, torn up King James Bibles, which he brought back to our table, saying, "Dad, teach me about

*Dad, teach me about Jesus. Teach me everything you know about God the Father and tell me about how He has been speaking to you.*

*Jesus. Teach me everything you know about God the Father and tell me about how He has been speaking to you."*

I spent the next six hours going from cover to cover through the Scriptures by the leading of the Holy Spirit, watching Zack suck up the truth like a sponge—it was one of my greatest days ever!

*Journal 11-15-2014 (Zack's Experience):* It will be the words that Zack spoke after our time together that will be with me for all eternity: *"Dad, I feel reborn all over again. It's like walking on air. Thank you for the best visitation I have ever had!"*

*Journal 11-17-2014 (Giving Thanks):* "Father, Lord, Holy Spirit, I have surely tasted You this morning in our time together. I thank and praise You for Your all-consuming love for me. I praise You for Your unexplainable grace, for being so intimately acquainted with me—for knowing my troubled heart, for knowing my fearful moments, for knowing all my days before there were days or nights created, Papa. Thank you, Holy Spirit, for allowing me to know the truth about how You feel for me, care for me, desire me completely, especially in all my weakness and unknowingness.

I felt our oneness this morning like no other time as I raised my limp and surrendered hand to You as any bride would when entering into the eternal covenant of matrimony. I now know that marriage is designed and created to feel like this morning, to be had and held by the Master of the universe, to be wooed and loved beyond all the doubting, beyond all the circumstances, by simply resting in the strongest arms of the loving Bridegroom Himself.

Sometimes I feel so unworthy of You, but this morning You showed me to be fully accepted and worthy for just accepting You and the things You say about me. You have made me new and built me up today. All I want is You, all I need is You, all I have is You. Jehovah God, I have heard from the Alpha and Omega this day and it is well with my soul. May Your divine presence flow through me all the days of my life, that I would never go back to a self-focused, self-centered life that leads only to the depths of death, doubt, and the destruction of my very soul. May I forever be used by You, dear God, to be a beautiful and wonderful vessel of the love You have for all those who know You and the ones that don't know You as I know You, Papa—not that I be seen or heard apart from You, but that You would be seen and heard and manifested in Your whole creation of the deteriorating world, may we walk hand-in-hand forevermore."

"Oh precious boy, you have allowed yourself to be influenced by My agape this morning and how I am well pleased and desire more of this garden-time with you, Son. Your tears of joy and gladness for just being with Me today is what life was always meant to be! The moments you feel completely overwhelmed and overtaken by My presence is the normal life in My Spirit-rest. Continue to take shelter under My all-consuming shade. Allow yourself to be fully given over and subdued by My uncontainable, overflowing love, whose desire is to consume you from the innermost part I formed within you, My loving Tony. I would move mountains for you, Son, and I have. Just open the eyes of your heart and I will show you things that are beyond glorious, that are over you and that I have placed within you the day I made you. Long before anyone was made, I was making and planning for all your days and our endless time together, dear boy.

It was My love that you felt, working out on the elliptical at the gym. It is the same love as when we walked in the coolness of the dawn of the day that I formed you and the same love which now is flowing through you. Let it flow dear child. You were designed for it and created by it. Love them, love them all the way I have always loved you. Go feed My sheep with the Love I have placed in you.

The love that you allowed Me to pour out through the core of your heart into the depths of Zack's heart set his heart burning with compassion and desire to be with Me fully. I touched the depths of his soul through the love of your Father and then I had Zack claim it as his own. As he confessed it to you: 'I feel like I was born again all over again, Dad.' That was most beautiful and this is the purpose and plan I have created perfectly for you, My precious lover. Be the vessel of My uncontrollable, unceasing, uncontainable, overflowing love."

I agape you.

Daddy.

※

# CHAPTER 12

# A Father and Son Walking in the Spirit with the Father and the Son

Shortly after returning from my November visit with Zack and after unpacking all that the Lord had revealed to me about the sweetness of our time together, I felt led to call the prison and speak directly to the warden about my time with Zack, to thank him and to make the requests known that had been divinely placed upon my heart during my quiet time. First, I wanted to see how to donate a dozen Bibles for that visitation room, as their Bibles were missing so many pages of truth and my Old English ain't all that great.

Secondly, I wanted to request more time for sweetness between a father and a son. Bimini and I had spoken at length and felt that this discipleship was going to lead to Sonship, which meant making some small family sacrifices and an on-going investment of both time and money. The R.O.I. (return on investment) would be monumental if Zack was willing to go all-in. After all, our kids and family are our primary ministry.

Initially, the warden came across as curt and unapproachable, but after I explained everything leading up to my visitation with Zack and sharing my heart for wanting to donate the Bibles for his visitation room, the warden's heart was softened by God. The one thing he told me about Zack that never left me was this. "Zack's a good kid, but he likes to talk on cell phones; Zack's biggest problem is that he is doing his time backwards." The warden agreed to allow me on-going special visitations with Zack; with advance notice and contingent upon Zack's staying out of trouble. I couldn't seem to shake this thought of my son doing his time backwards.

February of 2015 came quickly and it was two weeks before my planned visitation when I received a call from Zackery, expressing his excitement and anticipation about our planned time together—a Friday, Saturday and Sunday for six hours each day. I asked him how he was able to call me and he said he was using his cellmate's cellphone. I immediately told him to get off it and stay off it, as he was going to get caught and rob us of our special visitation by once again putting the glass between us. I reminded him of God's eternal law of reaping more than you sow and longer than you sow. There is always a consequence tied to our poor choices.

Within a week of our planned visit, I received a call from his unit manager. She said how regretful she was to give me the news that Zack was in trouble again and how he desperately wanted her to call to tell me that I had "jinxed him." She said she didn't know what that meant, but this meant we lost our special face-to-face visitation. The prison would only allow visitation on Saturday and Sunday behind the glass. She also mentioned that Zack would be transferred to a higher, maximum-security facility following their investigation. I apologized for Zack's poor choice and explained the whole jinx thing. I asked her how I could be in prayer for her and she said that she was good.

It was Friday morning. All prayed up by the mighty men of my Friday morning men's group, I headed for the Sarasota Airport to fly to Oklahoma and see my beautiful Zack. I had arrived at the airport with time to linger beside the aquarium just outside security. As I gazed at the graceful and elegant movement of the fish and their independently brilliant facets of color, I couldn't help being drawn into the arms of God, where I found myself praising Him for the uniqueness of each species represented. I commented to the gentleman next to me, "how majestic they are."

He was a bit uncertain and taken aback by my comment, but

soon fell in agreement and said, "Yes, they are majestic and beautifully created, aren't they?"

As I began to be ushered into prayer and captured by God's grace, He spoke clearly to me, saying: "light shined."

I asked, "What light shined, Papa? Your light shines in and through me; yes, I understand. Tell me more." But I didn't hear another word from the Lord. I quickly jotted it down in my journal and headed through security to meet my plane for Atlanta.

Once I settled on the plane, I felt drawn, as I often do, to go deeper. So I took the thought captive as I pondered to myself, "How many times can that phrase "light shined" be used throughout the Scriptures?" I did a quick topical search and found it only appears about a dozen or so times in both the Old and New Testament. I began to dig in, starting in Ezekiel and ending in the book of Acts— journal out and pen in hand, waiting with an expectant heart for a nudge from the Holy Spirit and the sweetness of His voice.

It was a wonderful journey within a journey until I got to the last Scripture reference in Acts 12:6-10 (ESV). As I began to read it, I was both overtaken and overwhelmed by the Spirit of God. Out of all the Scriptures, and out of all the settings within the Bible, this simple topical search of the phrase "light shined" was how God divinely guided me to:

"Now when Herod was about to bring him out, on that very night, Peter was sleeping between two soldiers, bound with two chains, and sentries before the door were guarding the prison. And behold an angel of the Lord stood next to him, and a light shone in the cell. He struck Peter on the side and woke him, saying, 'Get up quickly.' And the chains fell off his hands."

I was in tears and I'm certain that the folks sitting around me were wondering what in the world I could have been reading that would cause a grown man to weep like a child. So many thoughts raced through my mind in that moment: "Lord, are you going to physically free Zack and allow him to just walk out of that prison? Lord, is this just metaphorical? A parable to mean that you are going to spiritually set Zack free? What are you telling me, Lord? What does this all mean?" When the captain announced our final approach into Atlanta, I was an absolute mess.

I must have looked like Moses coming off Mount Sinai as I walked to the gate of my Atlanta-Tulsa flight. God had truly stunned me with this vision of a prisoner set free. When I got settled on my final leg into Tulsa; just a day away from seeing my precious son, I was awakened to the reality and revelation that God was giving me the very things He would have me pour out into Zack's soul—the truths poured out from the Heavenly Father into the only begotten Son. From the Son of God into a father and from a father into a son. There is such a beautiful flow in this divine vine of life; I was learning to trust and abide in all of it. It was in the trusting part that seemed to draw me deeper, not in the sense of having to try harder to muster up a message, but in a letting go and trusting into something unseen but completely present.

As I pressed into the Lord, I was divinely led to read the first six or seven chapters of the book of Matthew, which I had read many times prior. But this time I just couldn't get past the Lord's Prayer. So I begin to journal the following thoughts and revelation from God, the very things created in advance for a father to pour into his son:

A thought to ponder: As I have been reflecting on Jesus' prayer in Matthew 6 (ESV), I believe it holds the key to the message of the Kingdom that awaits us. Jesus said, *"Your Kingdom come, Your will be done on earth as it is in Heaven."* He had taught that when the Kingdom drew near to the hurting, the helpless, the brokenhearted, or the blinded, they were physically and spiritually healed and set free from the demons that kept them in bondage to the world. All chains were broken and break through was released and imparted (Matthew 4:23). Jesus shows us clearly that within the Kingdom there is perfect provision for everything required for life: an eternal well, a spring bubbling up from which to draw living water, flowing and poured-out, one which can and will quench any and every thirst for all of eternity (Matthew 6:33; John 4:13-14; 7:38).

I just couldn't shake this scripture, it would not leave me. "Your Kingdom come, Your will be done on earth as it is in Heaven." Is there pestilence in Heaven I thought to myself? Surely not. Are there terminally ill and sick people in Heaven? No, I can't imagine so. Are there demons tormenting and taking captive the very children of God in Heaven? No, certainly not. Is there any starvation, homelessness, nakedness, or a lack of God's provision in Heaven? Absolutely no way!

So, *Your Kingdom come and Your will be done here as it is in Heaven,* can only mean that what it is like in Heaven will be divinely manifested and imparted here on earth. Right? If so, would it be safe to assume that God's will is for His children to be conformed and transformed into the very likeness and character of His only begotten Son, Jesus—as image bearers? If so, God's desire must clearly be for the earth to reflect Heaven; that His ways and the ways of His Kingdom are to be shared with all His creation.

How, Papa? How can this be?

"*Through you in Me.*"

I was led to the book of Luke. "*The Kingdom of God is not coming in ways that can be observed, nor will they say, 'Look, here it is!' or "There!' for behold, the Kingdom of God is in the midst of you*" —Luke 17:20b-21 (ESV). Behold, through you and me, the Kingdom of God is released. The Kingdom is within us!

We can release heaven on earth. We are the branches of the living vine who bear the fruit of Spirit for the Kingdom of our Heavenly Father. We are the poured-out ones, vessels of His righteousness and holiness and created to be His very salt and light to the world (John 15; Matthew 5:13-16).

In surrendering our life (the self-life) to Christ for a life in Christ, I realized that we had actually switched kingdoms. We were once in bondage to the worldly kingdom of darkness as children of wrath and darkened in our understanding. Now we've been brought into the marvelous Kingdom of light as adopted sons and daughters—co-heirs with the Son of God. We are Christ-ones, now called to be poured-out vessels of this Kingdom, allowing the divine flow of living water within to become the splash zone of the love, light, and life of Jesus. We are like a river that actually pushes back the kingdom of darkness in order that the Kingdom of Light may be fully exposed and manifested here on Earth—yes, Heaven on Earth. In this exchanged co-crucified life we now get to be the cooperation of His operation, the receptivity of His activity in us, as us, and through us. Co-laborers in union with Christ Jesus. We live to reflect His love, wisdom, and truth to anyone within the circles of influence He has allowed each of us, in order to release His Kingdom into our marriages, our children, our families, our workplaces and every hurting, helpless sheep found to be Shepherdless. This is the normal Christian life.

I am convinced that this life within the Son it is not about a destination called Heaven, but rather about tasting God's goodness along this journey called life in Christ. On our worst days, amongst our most assuredly promised impossible circumstances and with the worst being known about our old dead selves, we are now walking in complete victory as newly-created, always-being-loved, risen, co-crucified children in complete oneness with the Originator, Perfecter, and Creator of our faith.

After soaking in all God had spoken into me on both legs of this

> In surrendering our life (the self-life) to Christ for a life in Christ, I realized that we had actually switched kingdoms. We were once in bondage to the worldly kingdom of darkness as children of wrath and darkened in our understanding. Now we've been brought into the marvelous Kingdom of light as adopted sons and daughters—co-heirs with the Son of God. We are Christ-ones, now called to be poured-out vessels of this Kingdom, allowing the divine flow of living water within to become the splash zone of the love, light, and life of Jesus. We are like a river that actually pushes back the kingdom of darkness in order that the Kingdom of Light may be fully manifested here on earth—yes, Heaven on Earth.

flight, it hit me like a ton of bricks. I realized in a twinkling of an eye what God had been trying to reveal and what the Enemy had been trying to conceal. It's a poured-out life.

A poured-out life is intended to receive what can only originate, flow, and be provided by the Holy Spirit within. This supernatural flow is from the Word of God which is living and active and sharp enough to pierce between the very division between our spirits made one with the Creator and our thinker, feeler, and chooser—the soul who has been taking instruction on how to live this counterfeit life from our mortal fleshly bodies since our inception.

The me, my, and I has allowed all of us to be deceived into believing we can live our lives backwards and independent of relation to the divine design of the Creator Himself—outwardly sowing and reaping from a darkened, fallen world. It is a helpless, fearful and futile attempt to find life through drawing from, sucking off, grasping for, and extracting from everything our fleshly bodies desire from the world in order to temporarily get our needs met; in order to preserve the self-life. This is deception at its core, thinking that our physical, mental, spiritual, social, and financial needs are all being controlled and provided for by the world and the one given temporary authority, reign over this worldly kingdom of death, darkness, and destruction. It is the perversion of our minds to think that we can actually find lasting love, joy, peace, patience, kindness, goodness, faithfulness or gentleness within this seen and fallen realm.

We were never created to live from the *outside in* as self-centered, and controlling separated beings. We were created to live from the *inside out* as generous Christ-centered, abiding, and derivative beings resting in oneness in complete cooperation with a higher operation, in a state of heightened intimacy through our receptivity to our Creator's divine activity.

The words of the warden rang through my mind in that moment: "Zack is doing his time backwards." The Holy Spirit was so quick and faithful to bring the truth to me:

*"Zack isn't doing his time backwards. He has been living his life*

backwards! Zack has been living from the outside in like you did for the first 46-years of your life, separated from Me. All of creation and so many of My children still choose to resist this inside out way of living for which you were created. Tony, you still choose to resist Me to some degree; you can't experience Life from the "I." There is no eternity in the "I." You can't find the freedom and victory I purchased for you at Calvary in the "I"." There is only apartness, separation, darkness, and ultimately death in the "I."

"Tony, My children have died to the "I" and are now alive in Christ. I AM and I will continue to awaken you and draw you away from the lie of the independent self-life and the lie of life apart from Me. I will continue to renew your mind with the truth that brings freedom as you allow Me to and to the degree you will receive it by faith as My child. I will teach you through My Spirit within as you confidently walk with Me and learn to rest, trust, and obey My voice."

As we arrived in Tulsa it became crystal clear to me what truth I would speak into Zack over this weekend visitation. I felt equipped for the world and as if I was literally walking 18 inches off the ground. I had truly been touched by God for the Divine things that were about to take place over the next 48 hours and for the rest of my life!

CHAPTER 13

# A Father's Spirit Encounter at a Rental Car Counter

As I walked through the Tulsa airport filled with fresh manna and on this mission from God, I felt way beyond good. I felt a peace and a joy I had never known before. I couldn't get past this message of living life from the inside-out. Living from the Divine Center within me made perfectly good sense. After all, the first verse that was ever shared in love and unveiled to me became my life-verse; from the heart of God and through the mouth of the Apostle Paul:

"I am crucified with Christ; nevertheless I live, yet not I, but Christ living in me: and the life which I now live in the flesh, I live by the faith of the Son of God, who loved me and gave himself for me.
—Galatians 2:20 (KJV)

All the spiritual dots began to connect, flowing from my heart into my mind. I realized in that moment that my mind was being renewed and there began a flowing out of truth from my Spirit into the depths of my soul (thinker-feeler-chooser):

"Do not be conformed to this world, but be transformed by the renewal of your mind, that by testing you may discern what is the will of God, what is good and acceptable and perfect."
—Romans 12:2 (ESV)

"So set your minds on things that are above, not
on things that are on earth, for you have died, and
your life is hidden with Christ in God."
—Colossians 3:2 (ESV)

"There is always a way that seems right to a
man, but its end is the way of death."
—Proverbs 14:12 (ESV)

"For my thoughts are not your thoughts, neither
are your ways my ways, declares the LORD."
—Isaiah 55:8 (ESV)

"Therefore, if anyone is in Christ, he is a new creation, the
old has passed away; behold, all things become new."
— 2 Corinthians 5:17 (ESV)

"Abide in me, and I in you. As the branch cannot bear fruit by itself,
unless it abides in the vine, neither can you unless you abide in me."
—John 15:4 (ESV)

"If anyone thirsts, let him come to me and drink.
Whoever believes in me, as the Scripture has said,
'Out of his heart flows rivers of living water.'"
—John 7:37b-38 (ESV)

"Fixing your eyes on Jesus, the author and perfecter of your
faith, who for the joy set before him endured the cross."
—Hebrews 12:2a (NASB)

"To put off the old self, which belongs to your former manner of
life and is corrupt through deceitful desires and to be renewed

in the spirit of your minds, and to put on the new self, created after the likeness of God in true righteousness and holiness."
— Ephesians 4:22 (ESV)

As I approached the Penny Rental Car counter I was greeted with the infectious smile of Ms. Tia. "Good morning, sir. Can I have your license and credit card?"

"Sure, Tia. Here you go."

"Florida!" she said. "Why in world would you leave paradise to come to Tulsa?"

"Well, when I got up at 4 a.m., it was 21 degrees at the Tampa airport and it was a balmy 32 degrees here in Tulsa, so I decided to head for warmer weather." Tia found that pretty funny. As we shared a good laugh, her smile increased even more. It was the most amazing smile I had ever seen, as she was just beaming with those bright white teeth and a joy in her heart that permeated the entire service counter. You could feel it from a hundred feet away.

"No, really, Mr. Murfin. What brings you all the way to Tulsa?"

In that very moment I clearly heard the Holy Spirit say, *Don't be ashamed, tell her the truth about Zack!* It was as if the Spirit was willing but my flesh was weak. There was a part of me that thought about what she might think of me if I told her the truth; that she would think less of me for having a son in prison. It brought immediate feelings of guilt, shame, and rejection.

But this time God got His way. I replied, "Truth be told, Tia, I have come to visit my son in prison."

"Oh, I am so sorry, Mr. Murfin. Where is he?"

"Boldenville," I replied.

"Hmm … Never heard of Boldenville, Oklahoma. Where is it?"

"It's about an hour northwest of Tulsa," I replied.

"I have lived here my whole life and never heard of Boldenville."

Then I remembered. "I'm sorry" I said, "not Boldenville. That's where Zack was before they moved him to Ominy, Oklahoma, about four years ago."

"Ominy?" Tia responded with great reluctance and a sense of uncertainty.

"Yes, that's it, Ominy."

Tia's bright and full-of-life smile was gone in a flash as her big brown eyes filled up with tears. She said in a trembling voice, "Dick's Correctional Center?"

"Yes Tia. How did you know? Are you okay, Tia?"

"That's where my brother is. He is in Ominy at Dick's Correctional Center. I have never been there to see him." She wept years of painful tears filled full of remorse, guilt, and shame. "I've never had the words to say to him. I've always been afraid that it would be uncomfortable for me and him both."

Tia and I shared life with one another for what seemed like hours as I stood at that rental car counter; God allowed us to pray and to encourage one another. I was floored at the sovereignty and omniscience of God and how He is always working and weaving things together for the good of those that He has called and who love Him. He is holding all things together by His mighty right hand and this God-encounter was no exception, as I thought to myself—*what in the world just happened? What are the odds of all this? What and who could manifest something like this other than the Almighty Father Himself? (Isaiah 41:10; Romans 8:26-28; Colossians 1:17)*

God began to speak these words of life:

*"Tony, this is the poured-out life we have spoken about—it's a choice to live from the inside-out. Living a life in-Christ is all about each and every choice we will encounter together as we walk in the moment. This morning you chose to allow Me to be seen and heard by abiding in My Spirit. I in turn, was able to use you to be My salt and light in Tia's life today—this is the normal Christian life which I purchased for you. Had you chosen to shrink back to protect and defend the "I" who has died and is a lie from the pit, you would have missed My blessing. This would have been a fruitless and lifeless exchange, (John 10:27; Revelation 2:20).*

I had a host of these God-encounters on this three day journey, each one as divine and further confirmation that Papa was at work and Tony in Christ was learning to rest, hear, trust, and abide in the co-operation of His good and perfect operation. It was the front desk clerk at the Doubletree Hotel, it was the valet, it was the bellman. It was and is everyone He allows us to encounter in this circle of influence called an abundant life or a Kingdom life – I believe all this for good reason. It's real.

# CHAPTER 14

## The Father Moving Mountains
## for a Father and Son

It's Saturday morning and I'm on my way to Ominy to see my beautiful son, Zack. I am just stunned by God and His goodness as I ponder and pray for this day of togetherness He has made and secured for His boys.

I pray for His anointing upon our eyes, ears, mouths, and hearts: that we would have His favor and experience Him with each of our senses and beyond. I pray for His every word to be spoken and heard in its perfect and precise moment, accomplishing everything He has intended since before time itself.

I pray for His protection against the evil spirits within those walls, lurking in the shadows of darkness. These same evil spirits would surely try to pull the veil over the eyes of our hearts in order to discourage, deceive, and blind the men of God from the truth of God. The same cowardly Enemy would surely oppose and attempt to rob and distract us from the divine time between a Father and His sons.

When I arrived at the prison, the line was out the door and so I waited and listened. What I heard was the same grumbling, complaining, and whining that God heard from His chosen race, the Israelites, who wandered in the wilderness for forty years. One drove an hour and this one drove two hours in an ice storm last weekend and that one drove four hours and missed out on this, that, and the other. This grumbling had gone on for about an hour before someone asked me, "Where you from?"

I was pretty emotional in anticipation of seeing my son and said, "I am from Florida and I'll be honest with you all. I would give anything to be able to drive an hour or ten hours to see my Zackery. As parents, we should be thankful that we can see them at all. We should be grateful that they're still here with us and we get to love them in this day." Well. A small revival broke out in the lobby of the Dick's Correctional Center, and it was awesome.

I finally made it to check-in and the female guard said, "Inmate number!"

I don't remember it," I replied.

"Inmate name, please!"

"His name is Zackery Murfin," I answered.

"Zack is part of an internal investigation and is on 24/7 lockdown. I am sorry. He is not allowed visitation. I couldn't help but overhear you say you've traveled from Florida. I know what a disappointment this must be."

I was shocked. I replied, "I spoke with his unit manager last week. I know he got into some trouble with a cellular phone but she told me I would still be able to have my visitation behind the glass."

"No, sir. While an inmate is on investigation, he is on 24/7 lockdown, making visitation impossible. Again, I am sorry, but I don't have the authority to overturn a D.O.C. regulation. Do you want to speak with the captain on duty?"

"That would be good."

"I'll call him, but I am certain that Captain Jones will tell you the same thing."

About twenty minutes rolled by before I was approached by Captain Jones. "Hello, you must be Zack's father. How can I help you?"

"I'm here to see my son. I had visitation approved by his unit manager a week or so ago. She called me to tell me Zack was caught with a cell phone and put under investigation, but she said she was aware that I had already purchased my flights and I would get my visitation with him, but it would be behind the glass."

"No, sir. She should not have told you that, as she doesn't have the authority to do so. Only the warden or the D.O.C. can make that call. I am sorry, sir. There isn't going to be a visit today."

I was heartbroken and Captain Jones could see it in my eyes. "Isn't there anything that can be done?" I asked. "I spoke with the warden back in November when I was first led by God to come spend time with my son. He's been doing so well."

"Yeah, Zack's a good kid. I know you spoke directly with Warden Brier. He told me that you are the dad who purchased all the Bibles for us, right?"

"Yes, that's right."

"Warden Brier is not here this weekend. He's actually home, sick. Do you want me to try to reach him at home?"

"That would be awesome."

"I don't think it will change things, but I'm willing to make the call." Within 15 minutes Captain Jones was back and said, "Warden Brier said to give you one hour behind the glass."

"Praise God! Thank you so much."

Zack's first words to me were, "I can't believe they allowed you to come visit me, Dad! That never happens in here." The second thing he said was, "Where's your Bible?" We were given not one, but over three hours behind the glass and I was able to share the truth about what it looks like to live from the inside-out, rather than from the outside-in.

We pondered living from the Spirit and provision of God; never from our flesh or the provision of this fallen world. We spoke about the Kingdom within and the river of life flowing freely from it. There was deep conversation about our inheritance of the Spirit—our source and supply for what we need to do all He asks of us. We defined our adoption by our Almighty Father in Heaven and His pouring into His always-being-loved, abiding children all He desires to be poured out of us as a drink offering to a dry and thirsty land. We spoke of life received and flowing abundantly into our spirit of oneness, flowing through our souls and poured out through our bodies so that the world might know Him who sent us.

As our visitation came to an end, Zack sat in awe of God and all the love He has for each of us regardless of our exterior circumstances, regardless of our poor choices and behavior. Yes, everlasting love on our worst day with the worst being known about us and still loved all the more.

As I was leaving, I saw Captain Jones walking out to the parking lot. I was led to approach him and thank him. "Captain Jones, I just wanted to thank you for allowing God to be poured out through a father into the life of a son today. I don't know anything about your spiritual beliefs, but I do believe you were used by God today for a greater purpose than any of us may realize. What I am trying to say is I think you stored up some treasure in Heaven today and I just had to say thank you from the bottom of my heart. Would you allow me to pray for you, Captain Jones?"

"Yeah, sure."

After praying, the Holy Spirit said, *ask him.*

*Ask him what?*

*Ask him if you can come back tomorrow.*

"Hey Captain Jones, I know I might be pushing the envelope, but my flight isn't until tomorrow night. Is there any way I could come back again tomorrow?"

"I don't see why not. Be here early, and I'll get you right in."

The next morning I woke up to a snowy blizzard. I headed right out to the prison and when I arrived I got in right away without anything more than a call over the radio. The stage had obviously been set by God. When I entered into the glass-encased room, there were two Bibles for our time together. We continued right where the Holy Spirit had left off on Saturday. It was simply God showing off.

Zack was facing all the windows with this thick, cold glass between us. He could see through the plate glass windows of the large visitation room behind me, which was a packed house. Beyond that, Zack had a great vantage point out onto the barbed-wire laced yard and saw that the snow was getting bad. I think he was truly concerned about me.

"Dad, it's really bad out there. Do you even remember how to drive in snow? I'm serious. It's coming down and I'm worried about you, Pops." I chuckled and then assured him that I would be just fine and if something happened to me I would see him on the other side. We laughed in confidence, with a great joy on our hearts.

At one point in this extremely loud sermon I had been preaching (If you've never been in a prison, the glass, is 3 inches thick and you can barely hear one another through the two or three small vented holes at the bottom of the window), Zack looked at me with the strangest look on his face. With eyes filled and tears of joy pouring down his face, he said to me, "Dad, they're all watching you!"

"What?"

"Dad, look behind you."

"What?" I replied.

"Look behind you, Dad. They're all watching and listening to you preach the truth!"

I realized in that moment that I had been giving a two and a half hour Sunday sermon to every inmate and visitor in the place and I began to cry and praise God. I told Zack that, "I guess we'll have to wait until we get to Heaven to see how He used all that."

Before I left, we made a commitment to write each other frequently in order to fan the flame God was working in both our hearts. We said our "See you soons," and I headed into a snowstorm with about 10 foot visibility. If I had been walking 18 inches off the ground Friday when I arrived, I had to have been walking 36 inches off the ground as I headed for the Tulsa Airport. I was praising God for an amazing journey and asking Him to help me try to absorb everything that had happened in the past 72 hours. I thought to myself, *This is just the normal Christian life—a Kingdom life stunned and awed by our good, good Papa.*

CHAPTER 15

# The Epistle of a Son Experiencing
# God in the Little Things

**February 27ᵗʰ 2015:**
"Dad,

Just had to start a letter to you! It's 3 o'clock in the morning and I haven't gone to sleep yet. Something so awesome just happened to me, I've got to share it with you. I started trying to go to sleep around 11:30 p.m. and have been tossing and turning so I decided to read some out of the purpose-driven book (ahead of my daily plan). Anyway, I read two chapters ahead of where I was and the first one was perfect because it mainly reflected off Job, who I was reading about in detail today and David, who I feel I'm a lot like. The next chapter is about baptisms, I realized I need to be baptized as soon as possible.

What I'm getting to is it was all things I've had on the front lines of my mind lately—the book was hitting the nail on the head as usual. After I was done reading, I was saying a prayer letting God know I appreciate Him being so right-on with me and not leaving any room for doubt. He answers all my questions soon after I ask them. Then, this is the part that blew me away—as soon as I finished praying, a chief officer was walking past my cell door and over the radio (used only for emergency security) said, "It's count time. 3 a.m., thank God!" Then the C/O whose radio it was, repeated, "Thank God!" I

111

was in amazement that they said those words over the radio. It almost makes tears come to my eyes how real He is, Dad. He is right here with me now, always. I am very tired, just wanted to share this with you because you're the only one who I know who can share in my excitement in simple little things like this. I love you man. I'll write more tomorrow. God Bless.

(Next morning) Today I found out the reason they said, "Thank God" over the radio. It was Daylight Savings and that extra hour they got made them thank God. Crazy though. Anyway, you said to write you and I'll write you back so is your pen broke, old man? I love you, write me back.

Love Forever, For Always, and No Matter What,

Zackery"

# CHAPTER 16

### The Epistle of a Son's Transformation Through the Battle for the Mind

**March 5th 2015:**

"Dad,

Just finished reading a chapter in the purpose-driven book a little while ago and it was right on time. I was having one of those days. Still locked in my little cell just me and Littleson; waiting to get shipped to another yard. I have been struggling with many issues (all unnecessarily) in here. I was just about to snap out and lose it when I decided to read chapter 11 of the purpose-driven book. Once again He hit the nail on the head for me. It was everything I've been questioning and fighting within my head.

Anyway, I've calmed down now and am looking through different eyes. Surrendering to God is a full-time job for me right now, Dad. I hope it will get to be a little easier as time marches on. Decided to do a little letter for you to let you know my mind is changing.

Each day I'm getting a little stronger for the Lord. Some days I'm getting a lot stronger. Like today. I am constantly struggling to resist all my old temptations. Not so much the drugs because that's getting easy, but the anger, the want for "self", the impatience and wanting to have material things. The list goes on a lot longer than that, I promise. But what is good is with these urges and slip-ups comes that little voice in my head saying, *Zack, if you're surrendered to Christ, why get mad? Why do you care where you are and what you have?* It's at times made me feel like I'm contradicting myself. But either way, I keep on fighting with "myself", trusting that it will get easier the closer I get with God.

Littleson says, "Hello and God bless." He is a little depressed today. It snowed and he didn't get the mail he was expecting from his lady.

PS: Dad, just found out the Bibles you donated got here. They wouldn't let me get one because I'm in lockdown but felt the need to come let me know they arrived. Nice of them, huh? Thank you anyway. That was really cool of you. The inmates will get fed and that's a really good thing.

I love you man. Tell the girls big love.

Love Forever, For Always, and No Matter What,

Your Son,

Zackery"

# CHAPTER 17

# The Epistle of a Son's Expression of the Co-Crucifixion of Christ

**March 9<sup>th</sup> 2015:**

St. Anthony,

Habakkuk? Wow! Dad, what is this book about? Scary stuff, sounds like vampires or something. Only have that same old half there Bible that I can hardly understand, but it is all I have and I have been trying to hike through some unknown parts of it. I understand that Habakkuk had a vision in his dream of all the wickedness, but God said for him to write it all down because it would happen one day, right Dad? I was just curious.

Well, here I am writing you like we agreed. I am still locked down 24/7 on investigation; just about sick of it. Having that visit with you really helped me, Dad. I was about to flip a nutty.

Thank you Dad, I love you lots.

What I wanted to tell you is, I drew a life-sized drawing of Jesus on the cross in my cell. Ask Warden Brier. It's awesome. I can't forget to say grace now, Dad. For real man, it's amazing. I folded up two mattresses and stood on them and had my celly trace my body, then I drew the cross behind him and turned him into Jesus. All the guards really like it and say it's lifelike. Call up here and ask one of them to take a picture of it and send it to you. The cross itself is eight foot tall. It is my way of expressing myself and the transformation God is doing within me, I guess. Also each time I think I got it bad, I just look up at His face and look into those eyes and remember how good I really have it.

And another thing, today they moved a guy in next door to me named Cross, isn't that crazy, Dad? He got smashed on pretty bad and had to get nineteen staples in his head. They put him on what's called administration protective custody. In other words the police are in fear for his life and no matter what he says, they're keeping him segregated. Anyway, I didn't agree with how they were doing him because inmates aren't going to believe that and he will be labeled a "catch-out," which will only cause him more pain and trouble in the future.

So when Cross started raising cain and kicking his cell door trying to get put back into general population, I started helping him by kicking on my door.

Then the active Captain came to see what the Hades was going on and calmed Cross down. When he was going back to his office and he asked while he was there, what I wanted. I told him I was just joining in because I was bored. He laughed and patted me on the head because he feels bad for me the way they got me in here on some innocent charges. Well, I stopped him as he was walking away and did like you told me to Dad, I asked him how I could pray for him. He said, "Are you serious or are you messing with me, Zack?"

I said, "I'm dead serious, I want to pray for you. Is there something special you would like me to pray about?"

He said, "Yes. If you want to pray for me, pray that I be washed with a pint of Jesus Christ's blood."

I said, "Okay, thank you." And he walked off.

Then as I started to pray for him, my neighbor Cross knocked on the wall and said, "Are you really going to pray for him?"

I said, "Yes I am."

And at first I thought he was getting slick with me but all the sudden he said, "Brother I know that I don't know you all that good, but can you pray for me too? Pray for my children and my family please."

I said, "Yes of course I can." And I looked at Jesus on my wall and began to pray for all of us and it was soon after I was done speaking to God that I realized how much influence I can have one way or the other in here. I can influence people for the Kingdom of God or for the world of Satan.

You were right, Dad. I love you man. Just wanted to share that with you, Dad. I miss you already.

Tell the girls XOXOXO and big love.

Love Always,

Zackery

## CHAPTER 18

# The Epistle of Reaping More
# & Longer Than You Sow

**April 13th 2015:**

My dearest Dad,

Thank God for your letter today. Wow, man I have goose flesh all over my body right now. I no longer than fifteen minutes ago asked our Father to please help me have some encouragement in my life. I am just overwhelmed with negative happenings since I've been moved back to this yard again. Your letter, that is, by my standards, a little late, gets slid under my door. I love you so much Dad and don't know if I'd be alive in here today if you wouldn't have led my heart to our Lord and Father. Thank you Pops, and Thank You Jesus.

Many of my old choices seem to be coming back to haunt me the more I try and turn my back from other inmates in here with me. It's like they see they are losing me and are trying to come up with everything possible to keep me down with them. Guess that's just to be expected, huh? It wouldn't be so much of a payoff in the end if it was easy. I just keep on laying it all on the line for Jesus and in the end I cannot lose. Like Matthew 10:39 (ESV) says, *"whoever finds his life will lose it, and whoever loses his life for my sake will find it."* It's kind of like I have to experience the bad before I can experience the good, right? That's how I see it. Dad, I don't question how the Bible came to be written. I just look at it like I read recently, it's my **B**asic **I**nstructions **B**efore **L**eaving **E**arth.

To answer your question from your last letter, yes I think you could come and baptize me. That would be the coolest thing ever to happen to me. I am in the process of getting approval for that, actually. Thank you for being willing to come see me and to do that for me, you're the greatest! I will keep praying for it and I am sure it will happen.

So you really think I will be an author? Or you know so. I guess I've never thought of it until now, but how cool is that? I have countless stories of miracles that Jesus has made happen in my life and in times when adversity seemed to overwhelm me. Yet through faith and encouragement from you I've made it to where I am today, safe. Although I've showed back up to Pushing to find my old mess still waiting for me, I have 100 percent faith and trust that I'll be okay and everything will work itself out in the end.

I can't even tell you how very badly I needed your letter to arrive tonight. Thank you Dad. You're a true miracle yourself. I have felt like giving up on myself and going back to hustling in here to survive and I keep on telling myself to be patient and wait on God. The blessings will come as I need them. The pressure is on me hard and heavy right now, don't be worried, but I will explain to you what's going on with me. Keep in mind that I'm a big boy and can handle it.

Look I went back to the yard I started off at in 2007 and I owe a guy here around $200 but here is the catch, he doesn't even want the money. No, he wants me to help him run his outfit in here. In other words, be his business partner and help him make more money. First of all, I told him I don't get money from the outside world and he said that's fine, he wants my help hustling people out of money in the world. He said I have the gift to gab and he could utilize my skills and that would cover my $200 plus give me some things I need. He had a good sales pitch, I have to admit but I stalled him out cause I don't want to call and scam people for money like he wants me to do. I just want to sit in my cell and mind my own business.

The whole yard is on lockdown right now so I haven't had to talk to him about it yet, but we are slowly being led back into normal procedures and I know he will be back on my bumper. He wants me to use his phone to call people on the outside and tell them I am the phone company or the electric company and tell them their service is about to be suspended and they can keep their lights on or whatever if they just pay ...blah, blah, blah. It's a lot of lies and I know better than to do that to people. What should I do, Dad? Should I do this one last thing to get out from under their thumb? I was just asking Jesus what to do and then a letter from Heaven arrived from under my door. So I'm asking you what to do.

I wish I had the money to pay him and buy the basic things I need in here so I don't owe anyone anything and I don't need to watch my celly's television or use his things or wear hand-me-down shoes. I look like a target in here, Dad! Like someone who "needs a little help," as they say. I hate this stuff, Dad!

The more I turn open my Bible and try to block out the games, it seems like all the more these lonely souls in here keep trying to find a new way to pull me back onto their side. Misery loves company. But I've dug myself a hole so deep over the past nine years that I'm afraid I'll never see the end of the suffering. You've saved me from myself in here.

Oh yeah, I have bad news about my health. I went to a State Medical Center to have my jaw looked at by a professional and he says I have a bone infection along my gum-line. He said that they didn't do the first procedure of putting my jaw back together right way back then, so now they have to re-break it, clean it out, and re-plate and screw it all back together again. I have six to eight weeks on an I.V. antibiotic drip in the hospital somewhere here in Oklahoma after the procedure is complete. On the bright side, I'll have a lot of time to read and write.

But Dad, since they have been denying me medical attention for about a year now, its gotten way worse than it would have with proper medical attention. Now I have to go through the trauma of this all over again. Do you think we could use this as leverage to get me out of here sooner? I told the doctor I wanted you to know about what they're doing first: this isn't right, Dad! It's not safe for me to be in here with my jaw wired shut. They denied me medical service over at Dick's Correctional Center and now it's all got to be done over again because of their negligence and shoddy botched surgery a year ago. This is one more of the problems I am dealing with. If I could just get out of here before I die or any of my family does, I would be thankful!

Kairos is a big thing I want to do this year and I hope to be in that as well as the faith program they have to offer here. It will more than likely be full of "catch-outs" and people just trying to get the certificate for parole, but like you said to me many times Dad, "I can eat the meat and spit out the bones." I like that saying Dad. Maybe you can call up here and ask about getting me into the next course of the Faith Program, it's a year long I think. Well Dad, first chance I get I will call you and talk so I can hear your voice.

I love you biggest! Please hurry and write me back.

Love Forever and Always and No Matter What,

Zackery

PS: Here is a drawing of God catching my tears; I got it off what you told me during our visit. Maybe save it for our book someday. You're so crazy sometimes.

# CHAPTER 19

## A Father's Thoughts & Reflections

**April 18th 2015:**

So many beautiful things God has showed me as I read between the lines of Zack's letter(s); so much hurt and pain, so much fear to overcome. I can't begin to imagine it all. All I can do as a father is to lean into my Father for what He has for me to do. As I reflect back on our sweetness together on the dock in my backyard, He said so clearly to me these divine words:

*"Just love Zack every way imaginable. He needs only love from the Father. Tell him how we spend time together. Teach him to hear My voice. He hears voices but often they're not Mine. I want to have and hold Zack like you do. Go, feed my sheep."*

I think about all the growth and fruit I have seen in and through Zack in just two visits of outpouring the love and truth of God into his dry and thirsty soul and I realize that he just needs more love, more truth, more light, and more life. I have been awakened to the reality that my son (His son) is being awakened to the fullness of a Father-saving Son, Christ for him, Christ with him, and Christ in him. A spark kindled within the depths of Zack's heart has now ignited a flame deep within my son and my part has become so clear—*"Go feed My sheep. Go fan the flame God has lit within him."*

My heart is captive to this transformation taking place in my boy. I can't escape the great depths of His love and the reality that Zack is being awakened by his Almighty Father—like a sleeping giant. The

Holy Spirit spoke these amazing words of truth through the Apostles
Peter and Paul and brought them to the forefront of my thoughts as
I read Zack's letter and penned these words today:

"To those who have obtained a faith of equal standing with ours by
the righteousness of our God and Savior Jesus Christ: may grace
and peace be multiplied to you in the knowledge of God and of
Jesus our Lord. His divine power has granted to us all things that
pertain to life and godliness, through the knowledge of him who
called us to his own glory and excellence, by which he has granted
to us his precious and very great promises, so that through them
you may be partakers of the divine nature, having escaped from
the corruption that is in the world because of sinful desire."
—2 Peter 1:1-4 (ESV)

"Now this I say and testify in the Lord, that you must no longer
walk as the Gentiles do, in the futility of their minds. They are
darkened in their understanding, alienated from the life of God
because of the ignorance that is in them, due to their hardness
of heart. They have become callous and have given themselves
up to sensuality, greedy to practice every kind of impurity. But
that is not the way you learned Christ—assuming that you have
heard about him and were taught in him, as the truth is in Jesus,
to put off your old self, which belongs to your former manner of
life and is corrupt through deceitful desires, and to be renewed
in the spirit of your minds, and to put on the new self, created
after the likeness of God in true righteousness and holiness"
—Ephesians 4:17-24 (ESV).

I can't imagine not sowing God's resources into such a hunger for
Christ as what I am seeing before my very eyes, and besides God spoke
these words to me specifically, "Love Zack in every way imaginable." I
have decided within my heart to send Zack the money and trust my
Savior for a favorable outcome.

# CHAPTER 20

※

# What the Enemy Means for Evil, the Father Uses for Good!

**April 28th 2015:**

Dad,

Thank you for the money you sent me. I am all clear now. I have some bad news today, I got jumped again pretty bad. I got stomped out by five guys and the first time they put me in the hospital for three days; then I signed a waiver to go back to the yard (general population) and when I went back to the yard they sent three more guys to jump me again. I am black and blue all over my whole head. My eyeballs are all the way red, hemorrhaged is what the nurse called them. I can't see out of my left eye. It will eventually be back to normal.

The good news is I applied and was moved to the Faith and Character program here on FC. I am so happy. It is a totally different lifestyle for me here on this unit. I am surrounded by people who want the same thing I want, "change through Christ." I am going to be all right, thanks to the Lord. I will heal up eventually and everything will be okay. I am truly blessed. I want to see you Dad. Please come as soon as possible. Maybe wait a couple weeks so you don't have to see me looking like I do now but please come soon. I miss you badly.

Can't talk about why I got jumped in this letter because it could be read by a staff member and I'm not going to accidentally tell on anyone so I need to see you in person. I am not going to use cell phones anymore so I filled out a phone list; it will be approved before long then I can call you. I put your cell phone number in the approved number spot so we will have to get money put on it eventually because it's either by collect or account and you can't receive collect calls on your cell phone I don't think.

I should be going to dental surgery soon. My jaw line inside my mouth is still building up pus. It is starting to hurt so I hope they see me soon. I don't think this last beat-down helped it any.

Dad, the Chaplin is new and isn't here yet, so I don't know if you will be able to come baptize me yet, but I do want to get it done soon just in case I don't make it out of here. I don't want to think of it that way but this last incident was the worst yet. I have never had to sit in the hospital for any length of time; three days opened my eyes and then getting jumped again was too much. I just want to be safe and get my baptism sooner than later Dad.

I am seeing life through different eyes now. I love you more now than ever, as I do all the people I've ever built a relationship with, but you more than any. You're so special to me Dad. You opened my eyes before it was too late. Thank you. God bless you, Dad! I am going to end this for now.

Love Forever and Always, No Matter What,

Zackery

PS: I suggest you read the book *Heaven is for Real* by Todd Burpo, awesome short story.

# CHAPTER 21

## The Great Awakening of a Son in the Midst of Trouble

**April 29th 2015:**

Dear Dad,

About to go into surgery, finally, I guess! I'm not really ready, to be honest. I don't have a good feeling about it. I prayed about it and put all my worries in God's hands, where I know I am safe!

I am sitting in medical right now, just thinking about life in general and waiting. I can't see too good out of my left eye right now, got a bunch of squiggly lines in my vision, it's crazy. I have to talk to you soon. We need to talk face-to-face before long. I am facing a lot of troubles in here, nothing to do with money at all. Just plain old craziness, Dad. My time is coming sooner than later I honestly feel and I just want to be prepared for it all.

I am all in with Jesus Christ and I know what He wants me to do while I'm in here. I do know this is where He wants me and needs me to be. I am just a baby in Christ but He has asked me to pass on what I do know to those in here who wouldn't listen to just anyone.

> *"There are a lot of guys who need to see me living from Christ. It's easy not to take the advice from a person who hasn't been at rock bottom and just thinks he knows how it is, but it's entirely impossible not to listen to a guy who you have been side-by-side with walking down the darkest alley known to man. I can get in places to spread to good news of Jesus Christ most people could never get to. It's my calling, Dad."*

He has led me to the *Faith & Character* program here. Although I have not yet been accepted as part of it officially due to the waiting list to get in, I'm still living on the unit and by the grace of God I will be able to remain on that unit until I'm accepted as a member.

There are a lot of guys who need to see me living from Christ. It's easy not to take the advice from a person who hasn't been at rock bottom and just thinks he knows how it is, but it's entirely impossible not to listen to a guy who you have been side-by-side with walking down the darkest alley known to man. I can get in places to spread the good news of Jesus Christ most people could never get to. It's my calling, Dad.

At times I get overwhelmed because I don't know a whole lot of Scripture yet; and I'm trying to learn and teach at the same time. I feel like a preschooler trying to teach algebraic equations. Some people look at me like I'm way out of my boundary, but most look and see that Zackery Murfin, a man who not long ago was selling drugs in here for money and hanging a needle out of his arm for escape from his own reality, is now on a righteous path walking hand-in-hand with his Savior, Jesus Christ. A guy not turning his back on the ones who are still blind as he was not long ago. I am showing them it can be better forever if they can just let go of the monsters of their past and present and grab a hold of the faith of Jesus Christ! If I can do it, anyone can. I promise.

I wrote this poem called *"Inside These Walls"*. I want you to hold onto it for my book. Our book I should say, we are doing it together as a father and son. You don't have a choice in it because it needs to be written before I get out. God willing I do get out at all. Nothing is promised as far as tomorrow goes, you know that.

I will be in the hospital on an antibiotic drip for six to eight weeks from what I understand so I will take that opportunity to write you as much as possible without boring you. I can't have my Bible but I can have a Bible. Hopefully I will get blessed to get one I can understand in normal English.

This last beating I took has left me half-gone in certain areas! You should see my eyes still Dad, they are blood red where the white used to be. Not like bloodshot red either, but like a vampire in the movies looks. It really brings out the baby blue in my eyes though. Guess there is hemorrhaging and the retina isn't fully connected, or something like that is what medical told me.

When Ms. Smith, my old case manager, called you, I was in critical condition, but asked her not to tell you because I didn't want you worrying about me. She can tell you how bad I was if you ask her, worst I've been so far in life. And you know I've been through the wringer before. To say it was intense would be quite an understatement. It was so bad that the prison said I had to sign a waiver saying that the Oklahoma D.O.C. wasn't responsible and couldn't be held liable if I got hurt worse or killed upon my release back into general population.

Then, when I got back into the yard, they got me again. They were scared they would kill me so I think they took it easy on me that second time compared to what they could have done to me. I was doing a lot of praying and I know that kept me alright. They kill people all the time in here, so I know God was on my side. I fought back hard on both occasions, but "strength in numbers" is the motto in here.

Now I am on the only safe unit for me but I know that will only last six to nine months. Then it's a flip of a coin for me. I've got rid of my pride and allowed them to keep me where I am. Old Zack would have already conjured up a plan and executed it to the best of my abilities. Someone would have got a beat down. But with Jesus there is no self-pride, only faith and trust that He will not let my enemies take me down. Part of me feels ashamed but I keep praying He will take that from me too. Without God I wouldn't be writing you today, I promise you that, Dad. I can't thank you enough for opening my eyes to Christ. Thank you.

I do want to ask you to help me get the things I need to lay down in my cell and keep to myself. I do really want a TV, hot pot, fan, and some good boots. It will be a pretty penny, Dad but I know what I need to be all right in here alone and out of the limelight. You can call up here and ask the canteen lady, Mrs. Brown, how much you would have to spend to get those four items. I still have the extra money you sent me on my books. If you can't, you can't and I do understand, it's not the end of the world. I'm just thinking about how to avoid situations best I can and that's by staying in my cell or in church, period.

Anyway, I've been in this holding cell for six hours now and I'm just thankful I was able to have pen and paper so I could get a good letter off to you. Tell Karagan, Kiah, Katalina, and Bimini I send my love and I miss them all and I hope to meet my baby sister Katalina someday. I'm thankful and grateful they are all saved and love Jesus. You're a good role model, Dad and I'm proud of you.

Well I am about to have to get surgery on my right hand for arthritis if I write anymore today.

Love Forever, For Always, and No Matter What,

Your Son,

Zackery

PS: Back from the hospital. They took a CAT SCAN and said my brain has bad swelling and can't do the procedure on my jaw until it goes down. I will be okay—thank God!

# CHAPTER 22

# The Saving Son's Psalm Within a Son

## "Inside These Walls"

Inside these walls I feel alone
But that's just not the case ...
Trapped in here so far from home
With many years to face ...
I could never do this time
and stand up to fight each day ...
If I hadn't met a friend of mine
Jesus Christ His name ...
He gives me power to carry on
Lifting the weight off my back
Of the guilt and shame I've built along
this long and rugged path ...
He walks beside me when I am strong
and carries me when weak in mind ...
Assures me I'm where I belong,
a place where light is hard to find ...
He knew He needed a soldier's heart,
one that can't be broken ...
To come in here and be a part,
of many lives that pain has soaken ...
Someone they would listen to,

a man who's felt their pain ...
And gone through all that they've been through,
but suddenly has changed ...
But only by the grace of God,
the choice is ours to make ...
Accept the truth or carry on,
to a life that only takes ...
Jesus Christ has gave His life,
so our mistakes can be forgiven ...
And on the Cross He paid the cost,
so our lives can all be liven ...
Eternally, so turn and see,
He's knocking at your door ...
You can learn from me all you need,
to fix a past that's torn ...
So inside these walls when you feel alone,
just know that's not the case ...
No matter how far you feel from home,
remember there's a place ...
In Jesus heart where you belong,
then eternal life forever ...
Make the choice, don't wait too long,
or some day could change to never ...

# CHAPTER 23

# The Epistle of Marcelo—Business Transaction Gone Spiritual

On May 22, 2015, divine happenings unfolded after a late afternoon business call from electronics giant Ericsson Electronics. It was a picture-perfect sales call with Ericsson supervisor, Marcelo Guerra, and I was certain that we would bring on a new tier-one client for His Company, Ground Zero Electrostatics.

It was late in the day and time for closing prayer with my team. As I begin to pray, the Holy Spirit took me away on a journey of thankfulness for the simplest things imagined, the things so often taken for granted and forgotten about: the air we breathe; the sustaining moment-by-moment beat of our hearts, the sound of the rain on our tin roof. I gave thanks for the richness of our relationships and the freedom to just commune with the Almighty Creator and lay our exposed and frail hearts in the security of His all-embracing, stretched-out hand.

Then in the middle of my prayer, Marcelo came as a picture rolling across my mind and so I began to give thanks for the Ericsson business opportunity and their imminent purchase order. I felt my soul thirsting for something more than another business exchange and then my heart was drawn to lift Marcelo up onto the Lord. I fell deeper into the Spirit and found myself actually petitioning my Abba Papa for something more than just the physical, something more than the gift of provision through another purchase order ending in yet one more transactional business relationship. I was asking and seeking fervently for a spiritual connection to manifest itself between Marcelo and myself; asking God for an encounter that would take us over into the spiritual realm; that He may expose the truth of why Ground Zero Electrostatics was created. Soon we were done and there was a sweetness in all of it that was felt by both my finance manager and myself. She even made a comment—"That was so special and so simple."

I was thinking, "Childlike," in my heart.

Here is the God encounter that unfolded and was birthed from a childlike prayer as my day progressed. Shortly after our end-of-day prayer-time, I moved on with my day and headed for the hacienda. When I got home to begin to unpack the events of my day with Bimini, I was alerted of new inbound email on my phone. This was what I read:

> *Dear Anthony,*
>
> *Thank you for providing the detail information pertaining to the labs, I am sharing the information with my boss to make the purchases as soon as possible. By the way, I love the Scripture in your salutation, and I myself love the Lord so much that I tabled my career to become a pastor. I'm currently attending Grand Canyon University's Theology Program in Urban Ministry—all for the calling.*
>
> *Thanks again,*
> *Marcelo*

Are you kidding me? Wow! I was stunned to the point of tears. I wondered to myself, "Why are you so surprised?" You prayed for this less than an hour ago. God is always listening and He is always speaking, why are you so amazed? Call Marta and tell her. She will be stunned with you." She cried to the point of having to pull her car off the side of the road.

The next morning I arrived to work and Holy Spirit put on my heart so clearly to take this spiritual encounter to the next level by simply inviting Marcelo into a much bigger picture, one I could not dream or imagine. *"Call and share the rest of the story with Marcelo,"* was the thought which illuminated my heart.

Below is the divine knitting I believe that God is constantly presenting to each of us as we just rest, trust, and become recklessly abandoned to His voice—yes, awakened and obedient in our faith as we hear Him speak to us. Oh, if we would just allow our Spirit to enter the playfulness into which we are all being wooed and summoned— God would bring us to places our hearts and minds cannot begin to fathom or conceive in the nature fallen realm we find ourselves. We were clearly created for something more, supernaturally more!

*Good Morning, Marcelo:*

*It was really awesome receiving your email yesterday, and I would like to reveal the other side of His Divine tapestry, the one not often seen and certainly one which is not typically discussed in the midst of a business relationship in today's marketplace.*

*A few minutes before receiving your email yesterday my office and I had just finished closing our day in prayer as we do to begin and end each day. As I was praying, the Spirit of God had me lift you up by name, as I gave thanks for our new business opportunity with Ericsson Electronics and the things seen in the physical realm. Then I seemed to lose control as I was drawn deeper into the Spirit and began to petition our Abba Papa to allow for a deeper connection between us in the unseen realm; for the eternal blessing of a spiritual relationship to be fostered between the two of us. Within minutes of arriving home, I saw your email come over my phone— wow. I could only fall to my knees in response and give thanks to our omniscient Savior, Jesus Christ—always listening, always speaking; always moving and weaving things together in our lives.*

*I obviously had to call the team and tell them how God was faithful to answer our prayers as I shared your email—you don't know any of us here, Marcelo, but we have been eternally knitted together, and you brought tears of joy to all of us, brother. Thank you for your bold and courageous witness for the Kingdom and for answering the call of God on the life He has given you in Christ the Son.*

*Had to share all He is doing in, through, and all around us.*

*Many Blessings,*
*Tony*

Thirty minutes after I sent the email (note: I did not *call*, as the Holy Spirit directed, but emailed him) I was notified that Marcelo was holding for me on line 1. *Yes, I thought to myself, he got the email.* We had a ten minute conversation with no mention of anything other than business as usual. My spirit was downcast. He then asked me if I would send him the product information he required for his bosses' approval and if I would send it via his business email; not the personal email that he had given me the day prior. I quickly asked him, "Marcelo, so did you not receive the email I sent you about an hour ago?"

"No," he replied. "That would have been forwarded to my home office mail. Why? What's up?"

I began to invite Marcelo into the story God had been divinely knitting together. As I read him the email I had sent, he began to weep over the phone and tell me how desperately he needed to hear all of this. Marcelo said, "I have grace-bumps all over my entire body." We began to share life together as I asked Marcelo what his plans were for ministry once he finished seminary. What was his deepest passion for serving and advancing the Kingdom of God?

What Marcelo began to share rocked me to the core. I felt the very presence of God with a half-written copy of this book manuscript setting divinely and directly in front of me—*A Father-Saving Son, the story of a prodigal of a prodigal.*

Marcelo said, "I have a heart for urban ministry but have no set plan in place. I actually have a deep passion for prison ministry and have felt grace-bumps all over my body like this only one other time in my life, Tony. It was years ago, when I was in prison" (I had to mute my phone as I broke into tears) "and I was given a radio platform to share the gospel message in prison. When I found out that it was actually being broadcast outside the prison walls and that my message was received and heard by those in my native village in Nicaragua, I felt these bumps all over my entire body, like when you just read me that email. You need to understand that I was doing four life sentences with no opportunity for parole and no hope for a future, but I had found Christ through all of it."

I had to stop Marcelo as I un-muted my phone (still weeping uncontrollably) so that I could invite him into the rest of God's story; so that he could see the other side of what God was knitting together. "Marcelo, in front of me is a manuscript of *A Father-Saving Son, the story of a prodigal of a prodigal.* You see, I have a 33-year-old son in prison doing twenty years on a trumped-up charge passed down by a corrupt system in Nada, Oklahoma, a system about which many books have been written, including: *The Innocent Dude,* by New York's bestselling author, John Grishum. My son Zackery has been in the prison system for over 10 years on an initial drug charge with a one-year county jail sentence."

We both cried from being touched by Heaven. As we stood in awe of God, Marcelo asked if it would be okay to write Zackery letters of encouragement and pray for a relationship to be fostered between the two of them. It was becoming quite obvious to both of us that this was a Jesus encounter—the divine workings of our almighty Father. I received this email the very next day after sending Marcelo a copy of the rough draft of this book:

Dearest Brother,

I am sorry that I did not have the time to reply to such a beautiful testimony and loving setting of God that's planted in your corporation. As I read the e-mail to my wife, I began to feel a kindred spirit and the agape love that Christ sent forth for us to exercise and fulfill here on earth.

I am deeply touched by the testimony God has given your family. Once I sat in a prison cell with four life sentences hopeless and in despair. I waited for nine years in front of a corrupt system that is broken and unfair. But God dislikes uneven scales of the law and His judgments are the supreme authority, even when we are sentenced to life. God revisited me at a due time, and overturned my case—His mercies triumph over judgment. As for your son, beloved friend, I'll keep him in my prayers from now on. I would love to write to him to support the feeble knees and give him hope with my story. God is not a respecter of persons and He can do anything according to His power that works in us. We are in agreement since we engaged in prayer that day that your son is being moved in front of the list to a safe place mentioned in his letter.

Please send all my love to your workers and family—do not forget to send me your son's information and as well as the pastors here that you mentioned to go to work for the kingdom. You are truly God-sent.

In Christ, For Christ,

Marcelo Guerra

"And it is my prayer that your love may abound more and more, with knowledge and all discernment," Philippians 1:9 (ESV).

To this day Marcelo and Zackery remain in frequent contact and are an encouragement to all those they encounter through the testimony God is writing. I believe this book will serve as a springboard for Marcelo's prison ministry that will be used as a vessel of hope and encouragement to set captives free around the world. It will be a vessel, which was always God's original intent by divine design. My relationship with Marcelo has fostered into an everlasting brotherhood, just as I had prayed many months ago.

Marcelo recently surprised us with a visit from California to Florida and we were blessed to meet his precious family and the newest expected addition to the tribe of Guerra. Our encounter in Florida was a celestial vapor, long enough to break bread together and have an hour of fellowship with my Friday Morning Men's Group. Who does this? I have never had someone travel this distance to share the love of Christ, but Marcelo did. We stand ready to follow one another as we each follow Jesus Christ on into eternity.

# CHAPTER 24

## The Epistle of Eternity Somewhere

**June 9th 2015:**

My Awesome Dad,

I love you man. I had an even more serious encounter with God, Jesus spoke to me today. I mean not like He always does but like I heard, felt and envisioned this: *"Once a man goes to hell, he will beg for the heat to be turned up and just beg for the memories of each and every chance you've had your whole life to change. To open your eyes to see after all these years of failure, I can't do it alone!"* Without Jesus Christ, I'm a failure and I promise you this Dad, I am not going to be the one burning up in hell remembering over and over and over, day-in and day-out for eternity each sermon, each word, each sign, each and every time I thought to myself, *Zack you need to stop this stuff and change your life around, you're a son of the King and you need to act like the son of the King, eat like a son of a King, sleep like a son of a King, and live out eternity like the son of a King!* I realized we are all going to spend eternity somewhere—it's our choice between Heaven and Hell and God didn't create His children for Hell. He created Hell for Satan and the fallen angels.

I love you, Dad. Forever and always, no matter what.

Your Son,

Zackery Murfin

# CHAPTER 25

## A Fire Being Kindled Within a Son

**June 11th 2015:**

My Dearest Dad,

I am on fire for God, man. I am so happy now. Come see me Dad, come see me soon. I want to talk and see you and share with you all God is doing in my life.

Things are so crazy here right now. The whole yard in on lockdown right now because there was twenty some odd stabbings last night. It was all over the news — "Riot at Pushing Prison." There were like fifteen ambulances piled in here.

I've been praying hard for Uncle Mark, praying he will get this fever like I have for Jesus. All I want is to learn more about the Father, the Son, and how the Holy Spirit is working in my life. Without Him I am miserable, I am trapped, I am addicted and afflicted. With Him, I am free, I am cured, I am blessed. No matter what, I'm a son of God, I am okay and on my way.

Everything may seem bad but it's not as it appears. I want you to come look into my eyes, Dad and see the light shining through them. I can't wait for you to be as proud of me as I am of you. I love you, man. I'm so glad you just kept on pushing me and didn't give up on me in here. Not long before the transformation I've had in my life I received a letter from you saying you received a word of knowledge from the Holy Spirit that your teaching and preaching were falling upon deaf ears and a hardened heart. But you kept on, and now I know it was what helped soften my heart. All that pride is falling off of me and fading away. I've even walked away from fights. That was so hard, just two days ago I did it, brother. I just looked the guy in the eyes and said, "God bless you!" And He did, because without God as my life I would have done what old Zack would have done and it wouldn't have gone well for that dude. Praise be to Jesus.

I am around meth every day, weed every day, cigarettes every day and my hunger for all those has just vanished. Just the thought of them leaves a bitter taste in my mouth—thank you Jesus!

Chaplin Fox is so proud of me. He always has good things to say to me. He told me from the way I get up and talk to the other 119 inmates in our class, he can tell that I may have a future in preaching the gospel. Ministering the words of Jesus. I don't feel like I know nearly enough to make a living of it but I do feel the urge to learn enough. He told me I just look like a completely different guy than he first met and he sees God all over me, inside and out. I can see and feel Him too.

Dad, what you did to teach my sisters a lesson was awesome. Wow. I could only imagine what was going through their minds as you got ready to spank them and then handed them the belt. I can't imagine the look on their faces as you told them that it was going to be too painful for you to spank them but there had to be a price paid for their offence and that they were going to have to beat you with the belt as you were willing to take the punishment they deserved. That's crazy. Good for you, man. You actually figured out how to inflict the punishment without hurting them. I have never thought about or heard of anything like that. You're a good dad and I love you!

I will write the girls sometime. I just really don't know what to say to them. I will pray about it and ask God what to say. Kind of like Marcelo, I didn't really want to write him back to be real about it. I love writing you but when I write other people I get writers block, it seems. I just don't feel comfortable with that many people. I guess it stems from being locked up so long. In a weird way, I am kind of anti-social. Not all the way but just in a small way. Shy, I guess, is a better description, I don't know what it is but I am going to pray about it and I will get over it, I'm certain.

Oh call Mom for me please. I wrote her a long letter about a month ago telling her what the Lord is doing in my life and begging her to ask God into her life and ask Jesus to be her Lord and Savior. She hasn't responded and I am worried. Please, just give her a call and ask her if she is okay and that I am not mad at her for whatever she decides but to please just write me back. I may just have to show her what Jesus has done in my life before she sees, it's the only way. Please do that for me Dad.

Father's Day is coming right up. I have a gift being made for you, but don't know how that's going to work out. I love you and wish you a Happy Father's Day right now if I can't get you out another letter by then. I don't have any stamps right now and I doubt I will be able to get any canteen anytime soon because I spent all my funds on shoes. But I can probably put in a disbursement and they will take it out of my trust funds. They do that for mail. When I get out, I will have a few hundred dollars saved up that they will give me when I leave. Could be a while but I will hopefully make it out of here. God willing, I will. I have asked God to grant me that through His grace and mercy so I do believe I will get out of here.

I love my new Bible, Dad, thanks! It's awesome. I gave my old one to a good Christian brother who recently found Jesus in his life. He loves it too! Dad I was wondering if you could buy me a *Strong's Concordance* that will go with my new Bible.

I love you Dad. God bless you and the family. I will write Karagan, Kiah, and KitKat when I get off lockdown. If you come see me, please call first due to the lockdown status because I don't want you to fly all the way out here and get turned away. One thing you don't even have to worry about again is me getting into trouble. I have laid that lifestyle down man, it's dead and gone forever. I live a new life in Christ just like you.

Love forever and for always, no matter what.

Your son,

Zackery Murfin

# CHAPTER 26

## Good Laughs and Peace Through the Storms

**June 26ᵗʰ 2015:**

Dear Dad,

Thought I would drop you a few lines, miss you big, Dad and I am learning so much. Actually watching the movie, *The Goonies* right now. Good laughs.

My whole life has changed. Inside first, and then outside. I lost my old life in order to receive my new life. Just like it says in the book of Luke. Have to say if it wasn't for you, Dad, I'd probably still be doing the same old stuff. Thanks be to God, I'm a new man. I hated the old me, Dad, I don't know how you ever stuck it out. I was a complete mess.

I've really been studying since we've been on lockdown so it was actually a good part of it all—like you always say, "everything for a reason, God doesn't waste nothing." There is always good in the bad, Dad, we just need His eyes to see it. Can't believe what happened here. We are just now starting to get up off lockdown for two hours a day. There were over 200 inmates involved in the riot. Eleven of them were almost killed. I think only one guy actually died. I have been praying every day for peace on the yard here at Pushing. Maybe you can put that in your prayer circle too, Dad, we need it here.

Hoped you liked my drawing, I really want your opinion on it ...

Can't wait to be able to call you and hear your voice, Dad. I love you, Dad and can't wait to spend time with you spreading the gospel and sharing our testimonies with people. Sure can't wait to enjoy life with you now that my body is filled with the Holy Spirit. We're going to have so much fun. Real fun.

Please call my mom and ask her to at least write me back even if she decides not to ask Jesus to be her life like I begged her to. I may have pressed it on her too hard, Dad. Now she don't want to write back because she thinks I will be disappointed in her.

PS: I've been setting my new Bible on fire Dad. I love it.

Love Always, Forever and No Matter What,

Zack

CHAPTER 27

# Putting Off the Old; Putting On the New—Ganged up with God!

**July 2ⁿᵈ 2015:**

Dad,

Another stabbing. Absolute craziness. Actually, several more of them. The blacks against the whites this time. A few weeks ago was the Indians against the Blacks. I ride with God now, so I stay out of it. I am free from gangs and fight a different battle that isn't against flesh and blood, but against the rulers, against the authorities, against the cosmic powers over this present darkness, against the spiritual forces of evil in heavenly places. The good thing about lockdown is I've had plenty of time to read and study my Bible.

Mainly so far I've only studied in depth Matthew and Luke but now I have started Romans and then I'm going to skip back to Genesis. I guess I'm kind of skipping around, but I'm making progress and having many revelations, and revelation leads to transformation. Isn't that what you say, Dad? Christians don't need more information, we need more revelation." Anyhow, I feel great. I feel that I am right where He wants me and when He feels I'm ready to leave I will. I am no longer a victim, I am a victor.

I can't wait to be able to get out and help people before they come to prison but I can help from in here too just as much, if not more. It's all for His purpose and glory. It may take a year and a half to finish the *Faith & Character* program here at Pushing if we keep on at this pace!

Lockdown, lockdown, lockdown!

I have to figure out where I can get some of my tattoos covered up or taken off when I get out. I have quite a few I want to get rid of. I just don't represent those hateful things any longer and every time I look at them I just cringe.

I joined a "Genesis One" group here that requires me to attend an above average number of Church services per month and

> *Isn't that what you say, Dad? Christians don't need more information, we need more revelation!"*

they help me once I get out to get hooked up with a good job, good church, all kinds of stuff. That isn't why I joined, because I know you will motivate me into attending more and more classes. Anything to better myself and get around people who want the same things— winner rather than a sinner. Tell the girls I love them.

PS: *"Do not fear what you are about to suffer. Behold, the devil is about to throw some of you into prison, that you may be tested, and for ten days you will have tribulation. Be faithful unto death, and I will give you the crown of life." —Revelation 2:10 (ESV).*

Love Forever, For Always, No Matter What,

Your Son,

Zack

# CHAPTER 28

# A Quick Note from a Son— Word of God, Speak

**July 29th 2015:**

Dear Dad,

I just wanted to send you a quick note to tell you how happy I am now. Thank you for not giving up on your prodigal.

PS: I just took this letter back out of the envelope I was about to mail as something awesome happened to me. I was lying in bed praying, and I asked God, "Father please say something to me, tell me what to do, tell me what not to do, tell me something, say something. If I had a son and he asked me to say something to him, I would at least say something." And I waited a minute or so and didn't hear anything so I opened my eyes and when I did, I mean the second I did, on the T.V. screen it said plain as day—*"no son!"* I guess He told me! The funniest part of it all was that it was on the Spanish Channel. Just thought it was awesome and had to share it with you—God isn't limited in how He speaks to us.

# CHAPTER 29

## Miracles Amongst Mayhem in the Circle of Life

**July 31st 2015:**

Dear Dad,

Man, right after we got off the phone it was a miracle! Do you remember praying that I would be blessed with the power of the Holy Spirit and have the ability to be used for healing people? Just as soon as we got off the phone, I went to a group of fifteen or so people and we made a circle, joined hands and each of us just asked for prayers to go out for our own little things, you know.

It got to me and I can't remember what all I said but some of it was, "that I feel God has me in here for a reason; this is where I belong. Jesus Christ has filled me with His Holy Spirit and for eighteen years I have shot meth; fourteen of those years I have done in prison. I have basically killed, stolen and destroyed my whole life; now Christ has transformed me so that all of you who have been watching me can see for yourself that God is all-powerful! If He can change me, He can change anyone. For all the lives I have destroyed, now I can be used to save lives through Christ." Just went on and on and the next thing I knew, a guy who has been saved for a long time, a guy who I go to for advice and questions I have about Scripture just started crying uncontrollably, and began thanking the Father and thanking Jesus.

Then, a black man who I don't know, a newer guy on our pod

pointed to me and said that he wants what I have; that he could see something in me and he wanted it. Then, the biggest drug-dealing, dope-doing, manipulating, tattooed-out dude in the circle just grabbed me and hugged me and told me that God has big plans for me and then he just broke down and said he's ready to feel what God has put within me. After I walked away from them I just started crying like a baby. I can feel Him, Dad. Thank you for not giving up on me, Dad. Thank you so much.

Love Forever, For Always and No Matter What.

Your Son,

Zack

# CHAPTER 30

A Prodigal Son's Repentant Heart —
Hungering for Righteousness

**August 5th 2015:**

Dear Dad,

I just got to reading Colossians and I had almost the whole book underlined. I underline all of the points I feel are important to continue digging deeper in my studies. I know it's all important but some of it really sticks out more to me.

I want to go over parts of it with you and that's why I am writing you back, even though I told myself I was going to hold out on writing you until you wrote me back—but I know how busy you are Dad with writing the book, serving in the mission fields of Kenya, running His Company at Ground Zero. I just couldn't hold off talking to you about how the Holy Spirit is leading me into understanding things—I wanted to see if you look at them in the same light.

I have *Colossians 1:9-14* underlined and that sticks out to me because each day I am growing in the knowledge of His will and starting to understand more and more how I should be walking as to please Him. It is strengthening me in so many ways. Being patient with my situations and circumstances and not only being patient but joyfully going through them; knowing I have received eternal life and I am able to be victorious in all the things I do.

I have also been delivered from darkness into the kingdom of

His marvelous light. It reminded me of the talk you read to me on perseverance. Because in here I really have to stick to faith, blind faith. This place is unlike any other I've experienced before—being in prison will want to make you give up. Many times Jesus Christ has been the only reason I didn't slip back into dead Zack.

Before I had Christ to hold me together, I felt as though I had nothing. Now He holds me together. *Colossians 1:15-17 (ESV): "All things were created through him and for him and he is before all things, and in him all things hold together."* Like Paul says somewhere else, when I am weakest, He is the strongest in me. I can't do any of this on my own in here. I tried it for four years in the Iowa State Penitentiary; now ten years in the Oklahoma State Penitentiary system. I can't do it on my own.

So I died and now it's Christ that lives through me. When I give up and realize I am nothing apart from Him, He is strong through me, leading me in ways that are above my ways and pleasing to Him. *Colossians 1:21-23, "I who was once alienated and hostile in mind, doing evil deeds, am now a part of the body of Christ ... blameless as long as I continue in faith without shifting into double-mindedness."* I understand what you were telling me all these years now, Dad, about keeping a clean conscience. Kind of like when you told me you couldn't help me by putting money on my books due to my drug habits—because it would make your conscience unclean and you would compromise your walk with Christ. I get it now. We all are basically building our spiritual houses. Our foundation is Jesus Christ. We are all a part of the body built upon a foundation of Jesus Christ. Built on the Rock and not sinking sand.

So this is my understanding. He is our foundation and each seed we plant is like a brick we lay on our foundation. Our bricks in the Spirit are of gold, silver, and precious jewels that will make it through the test of fire it talks about in 1 Corinthians 3, and those would represent our "good works." Our works done in the flesh produce bricks of wood, hay, and straw. They will burn up in the fire so we can't be shifty or double-minded into believing we can do anything apart from the Spirit. We must remain stable and steadfast in the Lord. In Colossians 1:26-29 it tells us we are rich with glory. Christ is in us. Christ is in me, right Dad? My part is to just keep seeking maturity, keep learning, keep asking for wisdom, and revelation on what I don't understand when trouble seems near—persevere!

He is empowering me as I learn and as I grow. Those are just the things I had underlined in the first chapter. I have all of chapters 2 and 3 underlined, and some of chapter 4. I am learning Dad and it feels great. I'm not into memorization yet, although you asked me to try and do what I can. I am going to finish reading the Old Testament first. I still haven't read 1 Samuel through the book of Esther or Ecclesiastes through Malachi, yet. I love learning and reading, am just not quite ready to spend all that time memorizing before I finish reading through the entire Bible first. I want you to be proud of me Dad, I will eventually start memorizing—I promise. I love you.

I still haven't received my copy of the manuscript, *A Father-Saving Son, the story of a prodigal of a prodigal.* I am worried that they kept it if you sent it already. Let me know, Dad.

Dad, I am enclosing a letter I wrote to Mrs. Leslie and her family—apologizing to them for what I did back then. I also enclosed her address. Please forward it for me so I don't get in trouble. Although I am finished doing the time for that specific charge against me, I want her to know how sorry I am. I want to ask for her forgiveness.

Love Forever, For Always, and No Matter What,
Zackery


*Dear Mrs. L,*

*I hope this letter finds you in good spirit and health.*

*I was wanting you to know that I am very sorry and remorseful for what I did to you back in 2006. I was a drug addict and had no direction in life. Now I have found Jesus Christ as my Lord and Savior and understand that He has had a plan for me since before I was born.*

*Although this prison time has been extremely hard at times, He has never given up on me. And it was in here that I finally received Christ Jesus as my life. It is no longer me who lives, but Him that lives in me, as me and through me.*

*I have been led by the Holy Spirit to inform you not only how sorry I truly am for the pain and suffering I selfishly put you and your whole family through, but that I am also a changed man and plan on ministering to kids like I once was, when I get out.*

*Hope you the best and God bless you and your family.*

*Full Heartedly,*
*Zackery Murfin*

# CHAPTER 31

### ✂

# The Father Training up the Mind of His Son's—"Tetelesti"—It is Finished 33A.D.

**August 20<sup>th</sup> 2015:**

My Precious Son Zackery,

I received your last letter and apologize for not writing back more often, it's easier to talk on the phone and it seems God has blessed us by allowing us to do that about every day—let me start by telling you that no father has ever been more proud of his son than I am of you.

Colossians is an awesome book filled with lots of golden nuggets of truth about our identities in Christ and the covenant of Sonship. It's really cool to see how God is growing you by leaps and bounds, Son. You have no idea how you're maturing in Christ. If I read one of your letters from a couple years back and compared it to one from today, I'd swear it was from two entirely different people—and it was. It's no longer you who live, but Christ who lives in you. You're a new creation in Christ Jesus, who has never walked the face of this planet before your new birth in Him. You see, Son, you and I were so bad off that not even God could *fix us*—He had to crucify us in order that we'd become dead to "self" in Adam, and alive to God in "Christ."

This is what all of Paul's epistles to the Church are about— identity, identity, identity! This is not established through *the power of positive thinking, behavior modification,* or the *will of trying harder to become,* but simply trusting in what we have already *become* by receiving a life in Christ. Now it's just for us to believe and receive what was finished (past tense) on the Cross of Calvary, and start walking out of our being, knowing we're complete in Christ and lacking nothing.

*Who are you in Christ?* It' simple! You are Jesus Christ in Zackery, and Zackery is hidden in Jesus Christ without one frog's hair of separation—a oneness by design and created for communion with the Holy Trinity, as we learn to rest and receive in this covenant relationship that has been bought and paid for. Until we can begin to wrap our wandering and untrusting minds around this kind of Sonship and our divine adoption (what it means to be sons of the almighty Father—Master Creator), nothing will make complete sense and we will continue to miss the mark, or not have a share in the fullness which was set aside for us from before "In the beginning"— the death, burial and resurrection of Jesus Christ.

Don't get confused with the whole "salvation" thing. Salvation comes by grace through faith—you and I bring nothing to the table but a limp and surrendered hand in marriage with our, "I do." God knew we were lifeless sinners in need of a Savior long before in the beginning, and He sent His only begotten Son so that whoever would believe in Him would not perish but have everlasting life! There is an epidemic of Christians arguing about who is and who isn't saved or born again, and they don't realize that this within itself is a scheme of the Enemy—causing the Body of Christ to be divided. Salvation is between each human being and God, and the only one who knows beyond a shadow of doubt is God—some things are just better left in God's more than capable hands.

You see, the crucifixion of Christ accomplished so much more than the forgiveness of our sin. Not that this wasn't paramount; it was awesome in and of itself. The blood and stripes of our Savior not only accomplished this, but His sacrifice also restored God's original intent for His children and the everlasting promise of a covenant relationship between the Creator and His created. It restored the covenant of Sonship, and so it reveals and restores our true God-given identities. Our identities expose our inheritance and our inheritance walked out unveils our destinies and purpose in *"Thy Kingdom come, Thy will be done."*

Sin is simple. It's merely an outward indicator of a deep inward condition that leads to death, darkness and destruction. It's anything we do to get our needs met apart from our life-source and supplier. The "I" in sin separates and simply means to walk independently of God and, or to miss the mark, or not to have a share in the Life of Jesus. Christ is perfection. He is the center and apart from Him we miss the mark of center and fall short of perfection—it is impossible to have a share in His life while walking separated and apart from Him.

This condition was brought on by the fall and the curse of a "self-life" or the "independent nature" as a result of man's own choosing against God's will. The fall of mankind in the Garden of Eden basically brought on eternal separation between The Creator and His created. But God being sovereign, loving, omniscient, omnipotent and omnipresent (all-loving, all-knowing, all-powerful, all-present) and much, much more—wanted us to know that we were created by love and for love. He is love and from love every good thing flows. It rules, as it is patient and kind, it's never rude or arrogant, it doesn't become irritable or resentful because it does not envy or boast in itself; it has no pleasure in wrongdoing, but is always rejoicing with truth; it never demands its own way. It's like His *word*. It never comes back void or empty but covers a multitude of sins—it bears all things, believes all things, hopes all things and endures all things—it never ends, and it never fails!

I believe we are always living, choosing, responding and filtering from one of two trees in our thought life—from *love* or *fear* and we know what God says about both—we were created exclusively for love, so *fear not*, as these cannot co-exist.

What is your value or worth to God? This is an elementary A-B-C, 1-2-3 building block to walking victoriously free in your God-given identity; so we must understand that value and worth can be determined only by what someone is willing to pay for something.

We will begin to understand the fullness and depths of our Father's great love for us; the immense value He places upon us and the core of our true identities as sons/daughters (created for a covenant relationship with Almighty God) when we begin to understand the unfathomable, immeasurable price that was paid for our ransom, freedom, and liberty.

The price paid was the most horrific, brutal and torturous beating and death sentence known to all the world—an innocent human man tortured and beaten beyond recognition, then nailed to a Cross for payment in full for you and me. Let this sink in! He died for your sins and for my sins. Abba Papa gave everything He had ever treasured, His only begotten Son (all man and all God) as a propitiation and payment that our sins could be forgiven, forgotten, forever vanquished and cast into the sea of forgetfulness (no, God's not forgetful). However, the forgiveness of our sins through the death, burial, and resurrection of Christ on the cross, as awesome and redeeming as it is, is not the entire *good news gospel* message! It is only half of the truth or half the good news that will leave you trying harder to fix yourself and performing more to make yourself right before God for all He has done for you. This is why the book of Colossians is so vitally important to me, Son.

I want you to look carefully at the tense of Paul's writing in Colossians 1:12; after all the things he was describing, for which they had been praying—"*And so, from the day we heard, we have not ceased to pray for you, asking that you may be filled with the knowledge of his will in all spiritual wisdom and discernment, so as to walk in a manner worthy of the Lord, fully pleasing to him, bearing fruit in every good work and increasing in the knowledge of God. May you be strengthened with all power according to his glorious might, for all endurance and patience with joy,*" giving thanks to the Father, who *has* qualified you to share in the inheritance of the saints in light. He *has* delivered us from the dominion of darkness and *has* transferred us to the Kingdom of his beloved Son, in whom we *have* redemption, the forgiveness of sins.*" —Colossians 1:9-14 (ESV)

This is a done deal and can be summarized in one word—*"Tetelesti."* The Greek translation is, "It is finished," an accounting term which means to be reconciled. As Christians, I believe we spend an entire lifetime pondering the fullness of what "it is finished" encompasses; I have chosen to believe for myself it is simply everything imaginable! This seed of truth leaves us with only one response to God, ourselves and others: "Be", just be who He has already created you to be in the finished work of His Son Jesus. As you read this, you must ask yourself this question, Son, "where is the Kingdom?"

Go to Luke 17:21 (ESV) and see what Jesus said: *"nor will they say, 'Look, here it is!' or 'There!' for behold, the Kingdom of God is in the midst of you."* The hope of glory is Christ in you, Zackery Murfin.

As we go back to Colossians Chapter 1 we can see the old made new. *"And he is before all things, and in-him all things hold together"* [you and everything else] —Colossians 1:17 (ESV). *"And you, who <u>once</u> <u>were</u>"* [past tense] *"alienated and hostile in mind, doing evil deeds, <u>he has</u> now reconciled"* [past tense] *"in his body of flesh by his death, in order to present you holy and blameless and above reproach before him,"* [past, present and future tense] *"if indeed you continue in the faith, stable and steadfast, not shifting"* [double-minded] *"from the hope of the gospel that you heard, which <u>has been</u> proclaimed"* [past tense] *"in all creation under heaven, and of which I, Paul became a minister"* —Colossians 1:21-23 (ESV). *"The mystery hidden for ages and generations but now revealed to his saints [you]."* *"To them"* [you] *"God chose to make known how great among the Gentile are the riches of the glory of this mystery, which is Christ in you, the hope of glory"* —Colossians 1:26-27 (ESV).

*It's finished (Tetelesti)*— so we must learn to walk in the completeness of Christ who redeemed us to be Christ-ones. We must be willing in heart to be the modern-day expressions of our Living, Loving, Breath-Sustaining Source and Supply for all who are willing to believe that in Jesus Christ they have died in order that He may live as Christ in us, as us, and through us. We must be willing to be called, to be surrendered vessels of His holiness and righteousness so all may come to repentance and know into Him who made us and took up residency within us as new creations in-Christ, 2 Corinthians 5:17. Forgiveness of our sins, yes of course! He had to make the temple(s) within which He would dwell — clean, pure, and holy. But you can clearly see the forgiveness of our sins is only a portion of the good news gospel message and it just keeps getting better.

Identity, identity, identity. This is what and where we should live from as Christians. We live *from* Christ as our center, right? Actually, it's better than that. You are Christ in Zackery Murfin! Blasphemous? No! If it was just about keeping Christ at first position, which would be a pretty flimsy doctrine—some days we'd be good and some days we'd be bad and some days would be really bad, depending on our ability to keep Jesus in first position or at center. This way of *being* is tainted with leaven. Can you see the lies that compromised the truth in this way of thinking? Just one degree off, just one little lie, brings on separation and places this legalistic yoke of nonsense around our necks, which derails us from His perfect truth. I understand idols and idolatry. That's not what we're considering here.

For instance, what if we allowed God to slip to 2$^{nd}$, 3$^{rd}$, 4$^{th}$ or 500$^{th}$ place? If He slips from center, (not sure what that even means) we will somehow feel that we're just not working hard enough to keep Jesus in His proper position. I know it sounds good to the flesh; it's just not what Jesus told us. The more I think about it, it's actually pretty ridiculous and wrapped in a nice little religious box that God can fit into, so we can remain in control. We can't afford to live by our feelings when God clearly told us that we are to live by faith.

Better example: what if life required considering our heartbeat as most important? Then what about breathing? Okay. Breathing is more important, right? I mean, we can't have life without oxygen. No; wait a minute; our circulatory system and blood flow should be first; after all, we can't have life without the blood flow that causes the heart to beat. You get my point. It's absolutely ridiculous to think this way.

> *We can't afford to live by our feelings when God clearly told us that we are to live by faith.*

Paul said it best when he said Christ had become his life. He said that he died and it's now Christ who lives. Paul had realized that the essence of Christ and the essence of Paul had become one. We were created to be poured out as a drink offering to a world that is dry, weary, and thirsting for the rivers of living water flowing from within Christians. As useable vessels of His righteousness and holiness, we can't help but be blessed to be His blessings to all those we encounter along this journey called life. This is normal Christianity—Christ in me, on my worst day, with the worst known about me, and being loved all the more by an all-loving Father.

Son, these are the truths God hungers to write upon our hearts. Truths that equip us and set us free to live and love from within Him. They are truths that will weed out and expose the underlying lies that the Enemy uses to taint, corrupt, and leaven God's perfect truth about the Holy Trinity, about you, and about all those around you. Satan doesn't have to get us off course by much. It is this *one degree* of separation from which Satan feeds, so we have to keep a clean conscience and a heart set apart and fixed on our Savior Jesus Christ. This is the Word our Lord has revealed to me as His messenger; but if I've said it once, I've said it a thousand times — don't rest in my words. Go to the Holy Spirit directly, who is faithful to guide, teach, equip, and yoke us equally with Christ, our Lord and Savior.

Son, you spoke out many beautiful things in your letter. I want you to know that <u>God is already pleased with you</u> and that <u>you don't have to do or perform to be pleasing to Him</u>. The work was already accomplished—this is my whole point above. It is no longer living a life of doing-to-become, but rather an abiding life at rest in just *being, in order to do!* Being, in order to accomplish all that He asks of us.

The problem at its core in Christianity today, in my humble opinion, is that many confessing Christians have not awakened to the reality that truth has set them free. They are free to just *be*; free from the deception of the self-life. I believe the Church puts way too much emphasis on Satan as our enemy. I am here to tell you that we have a far greater adversary.

Our bigger threat today is: "I," "Me," and "My." This is the biggest hindrance and stumbling block to walking out the victorious Christian life. The truth is, "I" died! The truth is Satan is a defeated foe. The truth is we're given dominion over the darkness. The truth is we have been given power over all the authority of Satan. When we choose to believe anything that is contrary, we give Satan our vote; and empower the lie which empowers the Liar! We are to keep our eyes fixed on Jesus—Savior-focused, not Satan-focused!

When we walk out the finished work of the Cross and the exchanged-life, we can be so free from "self" that we're set free from everyone around us. We are free from insult and offense, free from being disrespected and made to feel embarrassed; free from shame, blame, guilt, condemnation, accusation, and inadequacy. We become awakened to the truth that the battle has never been against flesh and blood (ourself and others), but we realize it's one being waged against the spiritual forces of evil, therefore, we put on Christ — we walk in and out of our Sonship. Our true identity can only be found in Christ. He is our way, our truth, and our life.

We also need to be awakened to the reality that as sons, we are also free from the trap of seeking the praise of man. I had to learn this through experience. It's painful to have your flesh stripped away, but it's part of His refinement process. Being *free* also means free from the more luring and self-gratifying aspects of the flesh—so we must remember that what is flesh is flesh and what is spirit is spirit. Therefore, we are also free from becoming prideful and puffed up by self and the praise of others. We are free from the need for accolades, envy, conceit, gratification, respect, compliment, honor, pride, praise, flattery and any approval from mankind. We simply get to give all these to the only One deserving of praise, glory and honor—He who lives within—King Jesus.

Some of these things feed into flesh and others condemn it, but in either case, although we all have it, we were not created to live for it or from it! We were created for communion with a Triune God, to walk with and live by His very Spirit. When we do, we will not gratify the desires of the flesh but we will have fellowship with Him. God says, *"For the desires of the flesh are against the Spirit, and the desires of the Spirit are against the flesh, for these are opposed to each other, to keep us from doing the things we want to do."* —Galatians 5:17 (ESV)

The Apostle Paul goes on to say, *"For those who live according to the flesh set their minds on the things of the flesh, but those who live according to the Spirit set their minds on the things of the Spirit. For to set the mind on the flesh is death, but to set the mind on the Spirit is life and peace."* —Romans 8:5-6 (ESV)

God equips us with more truth about flesh in 2 Corinthians 10:3-6 ESV: *"For though we walk in the flesh, we do not war according to the flesh. For the weapons of our warfare are not carnal, but mighty in God for pulling down strongholds, casting down arguments and every lofty thing that"* [exalts itself] *"is raised up"* [reasons against] *"against the knowledge of God, bringing every thought into captivity to the obedience of Christ."*

> *Warning, Satan's objective: "to remove Christ from the forefront of our consciousness and limit Him to our rational thinking and logical understanding; therefore separating us in our own minds."*

*Warning:* Satan, the Liar, Thief, Tempter, Accuser, Deceiver and Counterfeiter; who comes dressed as an angel of light, is always (24/7) trying to lure us into our flesh in order to get our eyes off Jesus (to remove Christ from the forefront of our consciousness and limit Him to our rational thinking, and logical understanding; therefore separating us in our own minds) and onto self. He accomplishes this through our thought life, the battle for the mind. Please understand this, Son. *Strongholds* are the places from which the Enemy does his exploits: killing, stealing, and destroying. These are the hiding places from which Satan attacks mankind through our thoughts about God, ourselves, and others.

Picture the Great Wall of China, or a fortress built-up around a castle being prepared for battle. This is the place behind which the Enemy hides safely, and from there he goes out to kill, steal, and destroy us. Strongholds are like great hewn blocks of stone (like those used for the Pyramids), and each represents a pattern of thought in our mind that Satan perverts, corrupts, distorts, or deceives in an effort to draw us out of the Spirit rest with Jesus and into our carnal flesh.

Through this deception we are lured by the Enemy to live from a separated pattern of thinking that opposes the truth—it's called our own understanding (self). But we're clearly warned in the Scriptures and equipped with the truth against this deception: *"There is a way that seems right to a man, but its end is the way of death."* —Proverbs 14:12 (ESV) Jesus gave us another truth. He said in John 14:6 ESV, *"I am the Way, the Truth and the Life."* Obviously, any way independent of *the Way,* leads to separation from God—Satan's end-game.

Satan's tricks are nothing new. He uses the same fallen patterns to accomplish this deception by raising up lies that are rooted in fear and contrary to the very truth and knowledge of God, hence luring us away from our walk in the Spirit into a walk in the flesh—from life to death. These thought patterns are often referred to as flesh-patterns or coping mechanisms that we developed early in our natural or carnal state, before we became born again—Tony and Zack (B.C.). Remember, the "I" in sIn represents the independent nature, the fallen nature that gets all of its needs met apart and independently of Jesus Christ our Maker, Creator, Sustainer and Giver of Life. The "I" in sIn kills. It is the flesh, and it leads to death, darkness and destruction but the Spirit of God brings eternal life, abundance, and peace—there is no other way.

This is why it is so critically important to know the truth that sets us free. We are told to *set our minds* and *hold our every thought captive* to the obedience of truth, remembering that truth is simply *what God says.* We must destroy the old ways of thinking and allow our minds to no longer be conformed and shaped by the patterns of the world, but that we would be transformed through the renewing of our minds to what God says about us, others, and Himself. Through this process we will begin to grow spiritually and discern what is the will of our Father in Heaven, knowing what is good, acceptable, and perfect.

This process of thinking allows us quickly to identify things that are in direct opposition to what God says about us and those around us, for we can't afford to believe things about ourselves and others that are in conflict to what our Master Creator knows to be true about us. After all, He did form us before the foundation of the world and knit us together in our mother's womb. Again, if we allow this corrupt way of thinking by buying into a lie, we empower the Liar and allow him to distort, pervert, and compromise our thought-life about God, others, and ourselves. Don't give the Enemy your vote. He is powerless against the strength and power of Holy Spirit that lives within us!

A wonderful illustration of this thought process of spirit versus flesh and the deception of our mind is found in the Scriptures in *Matthew 16:13-24*. Our brother in the Lord, the Apostle Peter, and the disciples were walking with Jesus on a journey to Caesarea Philippi. Jesus asked His disciples this question, *Who do people say I am?"* And they told Him, John the Baptist ... Elijah ... Jeremiah ... one of the Prophets ... And then Jesus made it personal by asking the question, *"But who do you say I am?"*

Peter, of course, was quick to answer Him, *"You are the Christ."*

And Jesus replied, *"Blessed are you Peter, but you did not come up with this on your own; but My Father who is in heaven revealed it to you"* [in Spirit]. Then Jesus explained to His disciples that He must go suffer things from the all-together religious people of the day (the elders, chief priests, and scribes) and be killed and raised again on the third day.

Peter was obviously batting .500, so he pulled Jesus aside and began to rebuke Him (never a good idea), saying, *"Far be it from you, Lord! This shall never happen to you."*

Jesus turned to Peter and said, *"Get behind me, Satan! You are a hindrance to me. For you are not* <u>setting your mind</u> *on the things of God, but on the things of man"* [in flesh].

To win this battle, we must know the mind of Christ through intimacy, by spending time with Him, by shadowing Him and modeling Him in all our ways. A life in Christ should look like Christ. We must have a tuned ear to the voice of God. He is speaking and has much to say to His sons and daughters. Jesus clearly taught us that His sheep know His voice—John 10:27. This clearly leads us to believe He speaks to His sheep. Destroying the lies of the Enemy comes by pulling down strongholds and, therefore, exposing the very hiding places of the Enemy in our thought-life. It comes by holding every thought to the obedience of what God says and through interrogating each thought that comes in direct opposition to the very character of who we know Christ to be. If you don't know Him intimately, you will lose this battle every time.

I believe it goes deeper than just holding a single thought captive. I believe we have to re-think how we process our thoughts so that they enter into alignment with the unseen realm. It is a way of thinking that goes far beyond the logical and rational thought process of the natural mind. This is because we don't serve a rational or logical God, but a super-rational, super-logical and super-natural God, whose ways are far above our ways of human thinking. I believe "setting your minds" means to allow the Truth of God to be the filter through which you allow every thought to pass. Let us learn together, Son, through another example of this found in the Word (found in Truth).

In Mark 8:1-21, Jesus and His disciples had been on a sailing excursion across the Sea of Galilee. Shortly after another Jesus miracle-moment and another bout of trickery by the Pharisees, Jesus and His disciples hopped back into their boat and headed for the other shore. Jesus clearly wanted to teach His disciples a spiritual lesson. He began by instructing them, "Watch out! Take heed of the leaven of the Pharisees, and [of] the leaven of Herod". —Mark 8:15 (BLB) The disciples began *reasoning* about bread. They had brought only a single loaf for their journey and so the topic of discussion began with their circumstance in the seen and natural realm (their logical

and rational thinking began in fear and flesh mode): they had no bread! Jesus heard their discussion regarding a lack of provision and saw a teachable moment. He said, "*Why are you discussing [why is it that you are focused on], the fact that you have no bread? Do you not yet perceive or understand? Are your hearts hardened? Having eyes do you not see, and having ears do you not hear? And do you not remember?*"
—Mark 8:17-18 (ESV)

Jesus reminded them of the miracles of feeding thousands, with provisions left over after all had their fill. Those miracles had begun with only a remnant in the natural, but in the hands of the Supernatural, fed tens of thousands. He asked them a second time and referenced the feeding of the four thousand; having seven baskets left over! "*And He said to them, 'Do you not yet understand?'*"
—Mark 8:21 (ESV)

Basically, Jesus was trying to deepen their relational-trust by changing their pattern of thinking to begin with Him as center, with Him as filter, with Him as provider. The leaven He was referring to was not literal; it was metaphoric, to mean: beware of the religious system (Pharisees) and the government system (Herod), because at their cores are a *self*-centered, *self*-seeking, *self*-reliant heart. They live from a carnal and *flesh*-centered, lifeless reference point—Self.

The bigger picture of what Jesus wanted them to understand is this: Humanity without Me, (Jesus Christ) as its center or core is demonic in nature. Thought patterns apart from Me are demonic in nature, as they don't originate with Me at their center! Any thought or patterns of thought that pass across our feeble minds that don't originate with Christ at the center are absolutely demonic in nature. We should be reminded of the voice of Christ, that said to Peter, "Get behind me, Satan. [You're in your flesh, living from the old self-life. Put off the old man and put on the new man.]"

When Jesus said, "Do you not understand?" He was trying to say, Have I been with you so long that your thoughts and patterns of thinking begin with what you don't have – really? Do you not understand Who it is in the boat with you? Is your attention span so short you can't recall the miracles I have been doing since I gathered you as a mother hen gathers her chicks?

Think about it. Jesus is trying to teach them a lesson about what it means to have Christ as their center, and they're thinking about what they're going to have for a mid-day snack. Their thoughts and hearts were inwardly focused, as they were being corrupted by the Enemy at their origin. The Enemy operates out of fear, so he used fear to blind them to see and hear in the natural instead of seeing and hearing in the spiritual — the eyes and ears of their heart. Their very first thought was carnal, as it originated apart from Christ Jesus with what appeared as their lack of provision and what they didn't have. All the time the One who dwells within us stood before them—none other than the eternal Creator, Provider and Giver of Life!

Matthew records that Jesus told us clearly:

"All authority in heaven and on earth has been given to me.
Go therefore and make disciples of all the nations, baptizing them in the name of the Father and of the Son and of the Holy Spirit, teaching them to observe all that I have commanded you. And behold, I am with you always, to the end of the age."
—Matthew 28:18-20 (ESV)

"Little children, you are from God and have overcome" [past tense] "them, for he who is in you is greater than he who is in the world."
—1 John 4:4 (ESV)

"He has" [past tense] "delivered us from the dominion of darkness and transferred us to the kingdom of his beloved Son."
—Colossians 1:13 (ESV)

"Fix your eyes on Jesus, the Author and Perfecter of our faith."
— Hebrews 12:2 (ESV)

Again, to the Galatians, God speaks through Paul:

"But I say, walk by the Spirit, and you will not gratify the desires of the flesh. For the desires of the flesh are against the Spirit and the desires of the Spirit are against the flesh, for these are opposed to each other, to keep you from doing the things you want to do." "If we live by the Spirit, let us also keep in step with the Spirit." —Galatians 5:16-17; 25 (ESV)

*Know the truth that has set you free, which is setting you free and which will set you free.*

Son, you are the hope of glory—Christ in you, as you, and through you. As we learn together to rest, trust, and abide in the living vine (the Way, the Truth, the Light), allowing God to be God as our life in the Son, we will naturally begin to hear His voice and will walk in the Spirit of Truth (Sonship)—He will produce lasting fruit for both King and Kingdom through our first-time obedience. Again, *obedience* simply means to *harken attentively* or to *listen under* the voice of the Holy Spirit.

I am very excited about what God is doing in you. Keep learning to just *be* the cooperation of His operation and life will be free and full of His abundance. Please don't rely on my teaching, always go back to the Holy Spirit (Teacher) and ask Him for your own personal revelation and the wisdom to understand the things He wishes to speak to you.

"If any of you lacks wisdom, let him ask God, who gives generously to all without reproach." —James 1:5 (ESV)

Love You B.I.G,
(**B**ecause **I** **G**et-to)
Dad XOXO

CHAPTER 32

# Thirsting for the Living Water

**August 26th 2015:**

Dear Dad,

Thank you so much for the *Strong's Concordance*. It's fun to study with. I also need a commentary to match my Bible if you can find one. The Bible you got me was an *ESV Crossway Study Bible*. Also what's up on the *Holy Spirit* book? I am thirsty for the living water! Can't seem to get enough of it and I am grateful to have so much time to study. Thank God I have this opportunity. Oh yeah, can you also look into picking me up a *Vines Bible Dictionary* too please.

Well I tithed to our Church here and am going to also tithe some to the *Voice of Martyrs*, just waiting on the response back from them with the information of where to mail it. I have everything I need right now so I wanted to give some to God's other children. I am so happy and appreciate that I have a dad that takes good care of me. Some of the guys in here haven't heard from their families in 10-15 years, no letters, no phone calls, no money for commissary, nothing. So, I feel it's my obligation to help when I can, any way I can. Even when it is just with prayer or words of encouragement.

Dad, good news. Right after we got off the phone form our last call and you prayed for me to be used more often in here for the calling of the Kingdom, it wasn't five seconds after we closed with that prayer they called Genesis One Group (a group of guys I joined a few months ago to fellowship in the Word). Anyway, my group of guys voted me to be the prayer warrior. I lead all the prayers. It's funny how God works, I used to shy away from praying aloud, but since I've done it more often I've enjoyed it more with each and every prayer.

Anyway, there was a guy named Camp, and he asked that I pray because they had denied his visit and told his family to go home. He was bummed out and wanted me to pray for his kids getting started back to school and doing well. His request was among many others but we all held hands and I prayed for each situation, including you being in Africa and your safety. Anyway, not even two minutes after I was done praying, not even two minutes, dad—a lady opened the door to our pod and called Camp and another guy to the visitation room. God has His ears directly connected to my prayers. Thank you, Dad, for your prayers and His blessings for strength. I love you, man; just wanted to tell you that. I know this letter will find you when you return from Africa safely.

Tell Bimini to write me back and tell them girls if they write I will respond. Don't forget to tell them I love them big.

Love you,
Zackery

# CHAPTER 33

## Angel's Wings Brushing Against Me

**August 28ᵗʰ 2015:**

Dear Dad,

I love you and I have really been missing all of you lately. Things have really been looking up for me now that Jesus Christ has filled me with the gift of His Holy Spirit.

I am level-4 for the first time ever, and that is the highest level we can possibly get. They have passed new laws of commutation in Oklahoma in an effort to free up the prisons—I truly believe it was done just for me, Dad. Thank you God.

Dad, I listen to your stories on the phone and I can only imagine how many lives Jesus will touch and save through us as a team. I can feel the angel wings brushing against me; sending goose bumps over my entire body when I just think about it! I start to think about Paul when the earthquake fell and the prison crumbled and he stayed there; the prison guard thought surely he had escaped, but he hadn't, and Paul yelled for him not to kill himself. He asked Paul how he could be saved. Not because of anything Paul said but because of his actions. His fruit was so powerful that it made those around him want what he had. Furthermore, his whole family ended up being saved!

Dad, together through the Holy Spirit I want to do the same thing because that's what God's telling me to do. He hasn't said a single thing about a job, a car, a house, a wife. All He said and continues to say each day is to *"Seek the Kingdom of God!"*

All I do now is study the Bible. I believe I don't have much time left in here, and what time I do have, I want to spend building my marriage with Christ. I want to spend time letting the current of the living water sweep me away. I'm all in! Psalm 139:23-24 says, *"Search me O God, and know my heart! Try me and know my thoughts! And see if there be any grievous way in me and lead me in the way everlasting."* I ask God these things, and He doesn't let me down. I can feel Him searching me, Dad. I cry out for Him daily, hourly and sometimes minute-to-minute. I talk to Him until I'm sure He is sick of my conversation. Just kidding, I know that He will never get sick of hearing my voice, and I certainly won't ever tire of hearing His.

Lately I have been really studying the law and the commandments because a lot of people in here try to hide behind grace. I don't judge them, but I find so many Scriptures telling me not to hide behind His grace. I want your opinion, Dad.

Here's a few of the Scriptures I've found:

"Do not think that I have come to abolish the law or the Prophets; I have not come to abolish them but to fulfill them."
—Matthew 5:17 (ESV)

"Therefore whoever relaxes one of the least of these commandments and teaches others to do the same will be called least in the kingdom of heaven, but whoever does them and teaches them will be called great in the Kingdom of Heaven!"
—Matthew 5:19 (ESV)

"And by this we know that we have come to know Him, if we keep his commandments. Whoever says 'I know him' but does not keep his commandments is a liar, and the truth is not in him, but whoever keeps his word, in him truly the love of God is perfected. By this we may know that we are in Him: whoever

says he abides in him ought to walk in the same way in which
he walked. Beloved, I am writing you no new commandment,
but an old commandment that you had from the beginning.
The old commandment is the word that you have heard."
—1 John 2:3-7 (ESV)

"But I say, walk by the Spirit, and you will not gratify the desires
of the flesh. For the desires of the flesh are against the Spirit and
the desires of the Spirit are against the flesh, for these are opposed
to each other to keep you from doing the things you want to do."
—Galatians 5:16-17 (ESV)

That's just a few of them, but many people in here manipulate
grace into doing whatever they want and think that's okay as long as
they believe Jesus died on the cross for their sins. Dad, I know that
from experience, but when I truly believed and received the gospel of
Jesus Christ into my heart, I felt a love for Him greater than I have
ever loved anything or anyone and so I didn't want to live that life of
flesh anymore. So, I feel like they are liars and the truth isn't in them,
just like it was for me before I knew the truth that set me free from
those lies.

I find myself on the battlefield each day I'm here, riding for God!
So many Scriptures call out to me now that the Holy Spirit is leading
me. Here are a couple more:

"The Spirit of the LORD is upon me, because the LORD has
anointed me to bring the good news to the poor, he has sent
me to bind up the brokenhearted, to proclaim liberty to the
captives, and the opening of the prison to those who are bound."
—Isaiah 61:1 (ESV)

"Therefore, do not be ashamed of the testimony about our
Lord, nor of me his prisoner, but share in suffering for the
gospel by the power of God, who saved us and called us to a

holy calling, not because of our works but because of his own purpose and grace which he gave us in Christ Jesus before the ages began and which now has manifested through the appearing of our Savior Christ Jesus who abolished death and brought life and immortality to light through the gospel."
—2 Timothy 1:8-10 (ESV)

Dad, I could go on for hours telling you all the ways God talks to me. I want to share with you a prayer I wrote the last time I ever used drugs, cigarettes, or any other dependency I chose over Him. It was back before you came to see me; I asked Him to help me and He did. He has filled my life with Himself. He has exchanged my addiction for a hunger and unquenchable thirst for Him and His ways. He killed all that old Zack, and now it's just Him who lives through me.

I love you, man. Here is a picture of Katalina I had drawn. If I had better pictures of the rest of you I could get more of these to you. I love you all. Thinking of you always.

Love Always, Forever, and No Matter What,

Zackery

# CHAPTER 34

## The Peace of the Father for a Son Amongst Chaos

**October 27<sup>th</sup> 2015:**

Dear Dad,

I just read something and it made me want to write you and tell you what it said. It perfectly illustrates the peace I have that surpasses all understanding. It was in a book by Lee E. Pollock. He is a Kairos volunteer here.

The book is called, *God is Not Fair, He is More Than Fair*. It's a book with several different testimonies, but the one I wanted to tell you about is of an art teacher who told his students to paint a picture of "peace." The first work he looked at was of a bright sunny day, the next was one of a beautiful winter afternoon; he looked at several that were all very good but then he got to one which illustrated several bombs exploding on what looked like a battlefield where people were dying, and it just seemed to depict turmoil and complete chaos. The teacher approached this student to let him know that he clearly misunderstood the assignment; the student replied, "No; I didn't misunderstand, look closely at the tree in the middle of all the chaos, there amongst its withered branches is a little robin singing with glee within that tree, I think that is the true meaning of peace!"

Dad, it reminded me of myself in this place. I'm that robin singing in the tree. All the chaos going on around me no longer concerns me.

People are forever asking me why I'm always smiling and I tell them the truth: God loves me and He loves you too! That's something to be happy and peaceful about, and I am proud to be His son and yours too, I love you, dad. I hope to see you soon.

Love Forever, For Always, and No Matter What,

Your Son,

Zackery

# CHAPTER 35

# A Son Crying Out to the Father— Praying From the Heart

**February 2, 2015:**

Dad,

This is the prayer I was telling you about the very last time I got high.

"Father God,

I ask of You, in Your Son Jesus Christ's name, that You take the hunger for powerless evil and wasteful addiction from me this instant! Lord, You know I am weak without You so I ask of You now to carry me, for I can't walk. Think for me, dear God, for my mind is of worldly things and material desires of no need. I've had enough, Jesus. Rebuke all thoughts I may have of giving into a grain of salt as my master. For You are the only Master my heart desires. I am Your slave and want to only obey one; You, Lord Jesus. My worldly addictions no longer have dominion over me. Thank you for not turning Your back on me as I have done so many countless times by enslaving myself to sin.

Thank you for Your grace and understanding. Unlike You, my Lord, I was brought into this world with a sinful nature and it's only through You, that I will be forgiven by our Father in Heaven. For You said, the wages of sin are death, my Father, and in Your son Jesus Christ my Lord I may have eternal life and the Holy Spirit to guide me along, and let me know there is always someone watching my back. Someone there to remind me when I lose my way in the wickedness of this fallen world.

Father God, I just want to ask You on this night, while I am alone in my bed and held down by intoxicants and overpowering temptations that You will have mercy on me, Father; me, Your favorite son, who is just an infant in our relationship but, Lord, by far the most driven child of Yours. I ask that however it is You decide to go about it, Lord, I am sure in my heart that You have already succeeded. I need You to remove these powerful urges to fall short and stumble into that quicksand that I have somehow been blessed by You to escape every time so far, Lord. I just know somehow that Zackery cannot do it himself. Without You, Jesus, I'm blind at best and very thirsty for nonsense.

You're my rock, my sword, my shield and the wheel that will drive me far, far away from all the Devil's tricks; from all deceit and deception; from the lies he is telling me right now Lord, as I speak to You. Place Your armor on me, Father, because I need it for all my days here on earth: my belt of truth to rise over all the horrible lies, my helmet of salvation to secure my mind of all I fear, the sword of the Spirit so I can be protected through You from the Devil and all his adversity; my breastplate of righteousness so when sin is surrounding me in this very dark and lonely place my heart will pump solid gold in Your name, Jesus; my sandals of the gospel to help me walk in Your word and live by the gospel so that peace will overwhelm my heart, body and soul far more powerfully than my addiction ever fathomed; my shield of faith, Lord, because without faith there is only a certain death trap awaiting me ahead. You are all I want, all I need, and all my tired eyes want to see!

I am no longer enjoying the darkness I've lived in all my past life. I am tired of the letdowns, the confusion, the way I passed up so many progressive opportunities, the hate, the greed, and the pride, Lord, that I've always seen as qualities of mine, but no longer. I now see it as a fallen bridge. A fallen bridge that now detours me to constantly take the harder way everywhere I go. I am just as tired as a man can be before he falls asleep, and when I fall to sleep, Father God, I want to go with You into Your Kingdom, into Heaven, into Paradise. I know I don't deserve it, but I just hope that You will spare me from an eternal life in Hell. I've come to see the Way, Truth and Light, Lord, and I'm ashamed of the way I have acted over the years. I want to walk as You did, Lord, so that I can live as You have, and always will. I want true joy and happiness to fill my empty life and all these things I ask of You, Lord Jesus. I also ask for my mother and brothers and sisters who are still living in the darkness—help them to hear Your voice even if You have to yell at them as you did me, Father.

Father God, all of these things I ask in Your Son's name, Jesus Christ Almighty. I know that You will make my request a priority because You love me so much. I realize there's nothing I've ever done to make You love me any less, and there is nothing I could ever do to have You love me any more—thank you for Your unconditional love and forgiveness. Amen."

# CHAPTER 36

# Baptizo in the Name of the Father, the Son, and the Holy Spirit

**November 2, 2015:**

Dear Dad and Mom,

I wanted to let you know that I received my water baptism and included my certificate with this short letter to tell you how much you guys really mean to me. I don't deserve to have parents who love me so much and treat me so well. Thank you both.

When no one else seems to care about how I am or what's going on in my life you are always there. Although you both are busy and probably don't have the time to answer my calls and write me letters, you do. When I've never done anything but let you down, you still put your faith in God and believe I can change.

You have countless times given me more then I deserve and all the words in the world couldn't express how proud I am to call you my dad & mom.

I love you more than all the stars!

Your Son,

Zackery

# CHAPTER 37

# Recommendations Sent Down From Above

**November 16, 2015:**

Dear Dad,

Just a quick note to tell you how I've been and what's been going on with me. Included with my update is a letter of recommendation that Chaplin Fox wrote for me. It's addressed directly to the court and the honorable judge who tried my case almost 10 years ago. Chaplin Fox is committed to mentoring me for my good and in order to help my case for a possible early release or even the courts revisiting the charges that were brought against me from the Tomahawk County Jail. Maybe there is even a possible appeal for a reduced sentence. Ms. E said she would talk to whomever and tell them how big of a transformation I have had. She wants the attorney, Mrs. D, to call her so she can answer any questions she may have about the change God has made in my life. Also included with this letter is my Certificate of Achievement for the Life Principles Course I completed. The Lord is doing so many wonderful and amazing things in my life, Dad.

My case manager said I will be moved to a minimum security prison by June/July 2016. So if I'm not out by June, at least I will be at a lower security facility that will be safer than here. Hopefully I can just stay right where I am (Faith and Character Unit) until I get out so I don't have to deal with any of the mobsters out in general population. I know God has it all under control either way, so happy days are here to stay. Or as you claim, I should say joyful days, because happiness is an overrated temporary emotion that changes with the wind, but the joy of the Lord is everlasting.

I got accepted into the Kairos program and will be going through this Thursday-Sunday. Super excited about that. This is like the Walk to Emmaus right, Dad? I am so happy and free, Dad, I am walking 3 feet off the ground at all times in here. I feel comfortable in the most uncomfortable situations because I know that when it feels like I can't take another step forward, I can just close my eyes and keep going because Jesus will pave my path.

Oh, yeah, I have memorized Colossians 2:1-7 (NKJV) so far.

"For I want you to know what a great conflict I have for you
and those in Laodicea, and for as many as have not seen my face
in the flesh, that their hearts may be encouraged, being knit
together in love, and attaining to all riches of the full assurance
of understanding, to the knowledge of the mystery of God,
both of the Father and of Christ, in whom are hidden all the
treasures of wisdom and knowledge. Now this I say lest anyone
should deceive you with persuasive words. For though I am
absent in the flesh, yet I am with you in spirit, rejoicing to see
your good order and the steadfastness of your faith in Christ.
As you therefore have received Christ Jesus the Lord, so walk
in him, rooted and built up in him and established in the faith,
as you have been taught, abounding in it with thanksgiving."
—Colossians 2:1-7 (NKJV)

It's coming slowly, but surely. It's taken me around two weeks to get this much but test me next time we talk after you get this letter, I would love to recite it for you, Dad. My celly is about sick of testing me! LOL ... I love you and all those beautiful girls!

Love Forever, For Always, and, No Matter What,

Zack

CHAPTER 38

# "You Will Seek Me and Find Me, When You Seek Me with All Your Heart"

**November 26, 2015:**

Dear Dad,

You wouldn't believe how excited I am right now! God spoke to me audibly, Dad. For the first time ever. It wasn't like I expected at all really. I was lying on my belly facing the wall sleeping during a count and at first I thought I felt a very, very soft touch on my shoulder, almost like something just barely brushing alongside me—but it woke me up and I had first thought it was my celly trying to wake me up for count, or to tell me that count was clear. I asked him,

"What's up? Is count clear?"

He said, "No, why?"

"You touched my shoulder, didn't you?"

He said, "No."

I laid there and thought for a second, "That's weird …" And that's when it happened, I heard crystal clear the words, *"spiritual test"* and I asked my celly, "What?"

And he said, "What?"

I said, "What did you mean by that?"

He said, "Mean about what?" And, honestly, I started to get mad.

I said, "spiritual test. What did you mean by that?" Long story short, my celly was asleep too; I realized that he didn't say or do

191

anything—God did! He spoke to me, Dad, it really happened! People all tell me it is very rare to hear His audible voice but, I did.

Now to what He said. Did it seem that maybe I will be tested soon or have I already been tested? I don't know. What do you think He meant by that, Dad?

I am going back to meet Kairos again on Saturday for a reunion, and I will be given a picture of all of us which I plan on sending to you along with another Certificate of Completion. I am going to tell them all about this divine encounter. I am getting so close with our almighty Father and Lord Jesus Christ. He is speaking to me, Dad. I have actually been touched by God. I am crying right now just thinking about it!

I love you, Dad. Just wanted to share the good news with you.

Agape,
Zackery

CHAPTER 39

# The Faithful Father Pours Himself Out as Truth Upon His Son

**December 2, 2015:**

Dear Dad,

I thought it would be easy to convince the blinded children of God in here to give up their ways for the ways of our Father, but it seems to be a struggle, Dad. So much resistance to going all-in. The Bible tells us in Ephesians 6:18-20 (ESV), "Praying at all times in the Spirit, with all prayer and supplication. To that end keep alert with all perseverance, making supplication for all the saints, and also for me, *that words may be given to me in opening my mouth boldly to proclaim the mystery of the gospel for which I am an ambassador in chains,* that I may declare it boldly, as I ought to speak."

There are a lot of men who say one thing and then do another. It is so sad, Dad. I feel bad for them. I keep trying to show them how much brighter and peaceful life is when we just rely on our Lord Jesus Christ. They are here on the God-Pod, so they fake it; thinking nobody is watching, but, oh, how wrong they are, Dad. *"They profess to know God, but they deny him by their works"* Titus 1:16a (ESV). They say they are saved by grace through faith and continue sinning thinking just because they say they believe in Jesus Christ they can do whatever they want, and I just cry because that is so far from truth. The Bible says in the book of Hebrews 10:26 (ESV), "For *if we go on*

193

*sinning deliberately* after receiving the knowledge of the truth, there no longer remains a sacrifice for sin."

It goes on to say in Hebrews 10:27-29 (ESV), "But a fearful expectation of judgment, and a fury of fire that will consume the adversaries. Anyone who has set aside the Law of Moses dies without mercy on the evidence of two or three witnesses. How much worse punishment do you think will be deserved by the one who trampled underfoot the Son of God, and has profaned the blood of the covenant by which he was sanctified, and has outraged the Spirit of grace?"

Scary stuff, huh? I am learning His Word (Truth) more and more each day and have so much to share with you, Dad. I get so excited when I discover Scriptures that fit the very things I am going through.

Dad, you said you hoped to be here before Thanksgiving but it isn't looking so good for me. It's getting really close and you haven't made it up yet, plus we haven't been able to connect on the phone, so I think this may be the *"spiritual test"* He was talking about. I just miss you so much, man. Hope you're okay and everything's fine with you and all the girls.

Agape,
Zackery

# CHAPTER 40

# Come Holy Spirit—Walk With Me ... Speak To Me ... Scribe Through Me ...

It was just a week before Christmas, 2015, and I knew that it was time to "Go feed His sheep." As I read through Zack's letters and pressed into the Lord for the words to speak into my son in this next season of life together, I felt this peace and prompting in the presence of the Lord just to speak out his release from prison in the upcoming year of 2016-2017. I began to envision what it looks like for a father and son to walk arm-in-arm through those 15 foot tall, cold steel, double-caged doors; to know what it would feel like the moment we pass underneath the large spools of razor-sharp barbed wire and out the other side. I am having unimaginable peace and comfort, knowing this morning that Zack has freedom and his chains *have been* broken off while on the inside of those prison walls. "*Freedom begins within,*" I pondered. Oh, what a thought sent down from above, and how it speaks to my heart and comforts my soul like a fresh drink offering from within the depths of a natural wellspring.

As I continued to allow my imagination to flow, I was reminded of a passage of Scripture God gave

> "*Freedom begins within,*" *I pondered. Oh, what a thought sent down from above, and how it speaks to my heart and comforts my soul like a fresh drink offering from within the depths of a natural wellspring.*

me while in Kenya, earlier this year. There I was in Africa, I had been pondering a very similar thought, searching for the words that could comfort and match the compassion I had in my heart for those beautiful little children of Kenya, yet feeling so inadequate for the journey ahead. In the book of 2 Corinthians it says, "Now the Lord is the Spirit, and *where the Spirit of the Lord is, there is freedom. And we all, with unveiled face, beholding the glory of the Lord, are being transformed into the same image from one degree of glory to another. For this comes from the Lord who is Spirit"* 2 Corinthians 3:17-18 (ESV).

I was ushered back in time to the comforting words of truth from several journal entries while on my mission trip in Kenya in the fall of 2015:

**Journal Entry - August 21, 2015:**
"Jesus And I Amongst The Villages In Kenya"

As we were walking amongst the Kenyan children up on Prayer Mountain, Jesus smiled; but I was overwhelmed and overtaken by the severe poverty. I was moved to tears of compassion, as my heart was breaking for each of them. I was astonished by their excitement to have something as simple as a large white man slip Jesus praise bracelets around their little wrists; with the intention to share the greatest story ever told—the John 3:16 story.

*Tony, I have called you to Kenya for My children. These were the ones I spoke to you about many times as we sat together and shared life and sweetness together in the midst of the garden. Don't be downcast in your soul. I have overcome all that you see, Son. This is why I told you to get out of your mind with only natural eyes to see what is limited and temporary. Walk with them today as I walk with you, Tony, allowing them to see into the depths of your heart and they will see Me, precious boy. I know, Tony; My heart, too, burns with compassion for each one. Remember, I formed every one of them in My image and I have a Divine plan and purpose for each, which you cannot see. As we walk as one today, I will begin to show you. I AM with you and they will know I sent you, as you allow the flow of My love to ransom their hearts son. Go feed my sheep and we will talk more, later today.*

Lord Jesus

**Journal Entry - August 22, 2015:**

"Jesus — Slay Me, Cleanse Me, Fill Me, Lead Me, Use Me"

Oh, Father God, there is such a heaviness on my heart for these always-being-loved children of Yours here in Kenya. Humble and break me anew, Father! Make me to be more like these meek and humble people of God; make me poor in spirit, Papa, as I, too, want to inherent the earth. I, too, want mine to be the Kingdom of God. Help me, Papa, to be pure within my heart! Speak Your words of light to me, Holy Spirit. Guide me; intercede for me, Holy Spirit. I need You, Jesus. I need access to Your strength. Please allow me an extra portion of faith, so that not one will leave unhealed or without what he or she comes searching for in this day; help me in my unbelief in this day, Papa. I feel so inadequate for all to which You have called me here! Oh, how my feeble knees get weak and my heart breaks for each one of them!

Come, Holy Spirit, fill the heart of your faithful and kindle in me the Spirit of Your love. Send forth the fullness of Your Spirit, that I can be created new for this new day and that You could reach and touch the hopeless and heal their infirmities. Make whole their souls and grow their faith through Your endless sea of miracles. Please, Abba Father, renew the face of Kenya and touch them the way only You can touch the inner depths of a man. Use my empty and willing hands, Father, to bring You glory. By the light of the same Holy Spirit that instructs the hearts of Your faithful, let me be wise and discerning within You, set apart for You; that I may enjoy and taste You today, Abba Papa. Apart from You, I will fail these beautiful souls today; so go before us and be with us so that our paths can be straight and well illuminated in order to bring You the glory, praise and honor only You deserve, Papa. Increase in me today, King Jesus!

*"Oh, My loving boy, I have planted the seeds of My Word deep within*

you and you have allowed yourself to be emptied so that I may fill you and pour Myself out through you once again, precious one. I have and will continue to awaken you, Son. Keep seeking Me with your whole heart and I will continue My Divine work within you, Tony, as you find Me. Oh, how I enjoy dancing with you, Tony-boy. You have My playfulness and joy within because you come expecting to find Me every day, waiting for Me when I pause and always ready with your quick "yes!" I love this about you, Son. You have allowed yourself to be gentle in heart. I still have much work to do in you, Tony; so it's okay to feel inadequate, unequipped and unprepared for what I call you to. It's normal to feel insecure and uncertain—many of My children struggle in the complete surrender and abandonment of their selves. Understand, Son; My life is easy, light and brings rest to your soul. Life of your own strength doesn't work. It's hopeless, exhausting and will always leave you trying harder to reach a destination for which you were never created.

Please remember, Tony, that your feelings are influencing your wandering mind, the very place from which I AM removing you. I AM training you to get far from your natural ways and the feelings that so often deceive. I AM with you to the ends of the earth and the depths of the sea, so let go and know that I AM ... I AM your God and you are My child. I will NEVER allow you to fall farther than My ability to catch you. Just continue to choose your words carefully and know in the depths of your heart I will keep you on the straight and narrow, not allowing you to stray or be deceived as you walk in My light. I will give you vision and guidance all your days! I AM the illumination of your path and feet forever and beyond My always-being-loved son.

Know that I AM adequate, I AM prepared, I AM secure and I AM always certain, so you don't have to be these things, as I AM these and more for you and all My children. Your part is to enter My rest, to abide in My shadows as my beautiful and glorious branch. Just be My lover and allow yourself to just be who I have created and am creating you perfectly to be ... Just be ...

Tony, can you feel Me right through you, pouring out these words faster than you can write or think? Your words belong to Me. Continue *all your days to use them as freely as you do. It brings Me great joy and gladness ... Now go! Go feed My precious sheep on that mountain and I will send them from the valley into your loving and capable arms, precious boy—love them well, love them all for My Father's glory.*

*I Agape you,*
*Yesuha*

## Going Steady With Eddy—You Do it Early, Daily, Dilligently and Yeilding

**Journal Entry- August 23, 2015:**

God laid this Scripture upon my heart in the still of this early morning, at 2 a.m.

*"That the God of our Lord Jesus Christ, the Father of glory, may give you a Spirit of wisdom and revelation in the knowledge of him, having the eyes of our heart enlightened, that you may know what is the hope of which he has called you, what are the riches of his glorious inheritance in the saints, and what is the immeasurable greatness of his power towards us who believe, according to the working of his great might that he worked in Christ when he raised him from the dead and seated him at his right hand in the heavenly places, far above all rule and authority and power and dominion, and above every name that is named, not only in this age but also in the one to come"*
*—Ephesians 1:17-18 (ESV).*

Holy Spirit, grant me the spirit of revelation and anoint my inner eye and ears to hear the depths of Your heart and the things You would say to me in this day. Why have You brought me to Kenya, Father? What do You want me to see? What is it that You want to say to me

*"You will never find in your mind what you hunger and search for in the depths of your heart, Son..."*

and through me, Papa? Offer me Your voice that I may know You in a deeper, increased way in this new day You have made.

I see You there, Jesus, in all that tall green grass blowing; dressed in that beautiful flowing white robe tied with a deep purple, silky sash with golden fringe tassels wrapped around Your waist. Your hair looks as silky as Your sash. Your face glows with radiance and life. Your smile pierces my soul, Lord, and I stand here in awe of You, Jesus. I come to You this morning with these questions; that we might walk together on the water of life. I know I was brought here for Your Divine service and I come with a heart to hear from You regarding the questions I pondered with Your Holy Spirit early this morning.

"Oh, Tony; you are something else, dear brother. You are always perusing My thoughts and ways and our friendship blossoms as a result of it. You seek Me and find Me each time because I cherish and desire our time together; more and more I hunger for this intimacy with you. I have bought you, and brought you to Kenya that we would have this time, a time free from the distractions of work and free from the busyness of life at home with family.

"What you are experiencing is a normal life within Me. This is the life for which I created you, Tony. I don't see you as you see you. I see your uttermost completeness within Me. I see you through the finished work of My cross, to which I AM awakening you. You can't imagine you yet, but you're beginning to see things as they really are when you open the eyes of your heart and allow your mind to rest. This is how you discern what I AM telling you right now as you pen My words in your journal. It's actually OUR journal and you don't completely understand or realize it, but there is union oneness in your writing and therefore we write together as I give you words to write. You're no longer in your mind, you're in your innermost parts, which I formed long ago; and your mind sleeps silently as you listen to My voice.

"You hear Me so clearly but seem so surprised by it all! You will never find in your mind what you hunger and search for in the depths of your heart, Son. Tony, you always have complete access to Me through your heart and your writing (our writing) because you write from the depths of your heart. I have so much to write through you. I want you to write everything imaginable. My skies and the Heavenlies are the limit! We'll write blogs and books, diaries and devotionals. Oh, will we write books!

"Now go. They're calling us to get on the bus and I AM with you as your heart is ready to worship with your brothers and sisters at IVC and the team I have formed for this mission. I have much to share. Just continue to trust Me with all your heart."

Love you big, too,
King Jesus

# CHAPTER 41

## The Calling of the Father Onto His Son ... Watchmen Of The Land and Lord

**January 4, 2016:**
Dear Dad,

Just wanted you to know how my week's been. Great! Dad, the C.H.O.G., *Christian House of God* asked me to be one of the ministers for its services. They asked me after the leader of the service kinda put me on blast and asked me to get up in front of the whole church and share the revelation I had with everyone. I was just asking *him* to share the message with everyone during *his* sermon and about half way through the service he asked me to come up and share what I had received from the Lord.

At first I wanted to say, "No!" I was kinda upset he would throw me under the spotlight like that, but then Holy Spirit said, "*Do it for Me.*" So I swallowed my emotions, and I began to walk to the front of the room and everyone started cheering for me. It only made my feelings and mind scatter more, but I kept going! I didn't have anything prepared, but I knew what was on my mind and how it all could be explained.

Once I got up there and everyone calmed down I asked them to open their Bibles and turn to Matthew 22:1-14: The Parable of the Marriage Feast. I pointed out first that Jesus started off by saying, "*The kingdom of heaven may be compared to a king who gave a wedding feast for his son, and sent his servants to call those who were invited to the wedding feast, but they would not come"* Matthew 22:2-3 (ESV). He even sent his slaves out another time but they again paid no attention. Then I explained that Jesus was talking about the Jews — many times God told them to come to Him but they rejected Him many times as you know from the Old Testament. Then God sent us a Savior, Jesus and He called all of us (Jew and Gentile) both good and evil, whoever would believe and have faith and receive the Gift. Then I read them, *"But when the king came in to look at the guests, he saw a man who had no wedding garment. And he said to him, 'Friend, how did you get in here without a wedding garment?' And he was speechless. Then the king said to the servants, 'Bind him hand and foot and cast him into the outer darkness. In that place there will be weeping and gnashing of teeth.' For many are called, but few are chosen"* Matthew 22:11-14 (ESV).

Then I shared what I remembered about the marriage of the Lamb in Revelation 19: *"Let us rejoice and be glad and give the glory to him, for the marriage of the Lamb has come, and his Bride has made herself ready; it was given to her to clothe herself in fine linen, bright and clean—for the fine linen is the righteous acts of the saints. And the angel said to me, 'Write this: Blessed are those who are invited to the Marriage supper of the Lamb.'"And he said to me these are true words of God"* Revelation 19:7-9 (ESV).

So we must ask ourselves, what are these *righteous acts?* They are our *"equitable deeds"* according to the Greek for *"Dikaioma."* So what are our deeds? Our deeds are the actual works that the Spirit of Grace (Holy Spirit) does within us as we learn to cooperate with Him. We have to remember we can do *nothing* apart from God, *but* with Him, through Him (Him-in-us and us-in-Him) we can do all good things!

Then I took them to Ezekiel 33:1-9 and shared with them about our duties and inheritance as His Watchmen. How we are to witness and proclaim the gospel at all times with our actions (works) and our words when it's necessary! Remember: *"Do you not believe that I am in the Father, and the Father is in me? The words that I speak to you I do not speak on my own authority, but the Father who <u>abides</u> in me does <u>his</u>*

_works"_ John 14:10 (ESV). And: _"If I do not do the works of my Father do not believe me; but if I do them, even though you do not believe me, believe the works, that you may know and understand that the Father is in me and I am in the Father"_ John 10:37-38 (ESV). Then I closed with:"_What shall we say then? Are we to continue in sin that grace may abound? By no means. How can we who have died to sin still live in it?_ Romans 6:1 (ESV). We can't!

That was basically what I shared and after I was done the whole place lit up! Chaplain gave me a high five and then the head minister asked me if I would like to continue to minister for them once a month or so to start off. Wow, I can't believe this is all happening so fast. Just a year or more ago I was shooting meth and running with gangs, now I am shooting truth and running with the most high Jesus Christ!

Praise God!

Love you, Dad!

Agape,

Zackery

# CHAPTER 42

## A Wonderful Counselor Within the Wonderful Counselor

After learning about the new commutation laws of Oklahoma, I felt led in February, 2016, on an early morning drive to work, to reach out to a Ms. D, a wonderful Christian attorney, whose heart is for the Lord and the justice, safety, and well-being of her clients. With all the recent promptings by the Holy Spirit to speak out and claim Zackery's God-given identity, inheritance, and destiny, I shared my heart as to Zack's amazing transformation in Christ and what I believe to be a calling on Zack's life to the Ministry — inside and outside those prison walls.

> *"I explained to Zack, this is how miracles take place: Choosing to believe and walk out of both the truth (what God says), and reality (what God sees), by faith (what is unseen, non-logical, non-rational, and incomprehensible in mind) —— all in order to release Gods blessing that originated in the throne-room of Heaven and flows down like living water through earthen-vessels with surrendered hearts. The cooperation of the man while under God's divine influence."*
> *——Living Naturally Supernatural*

After much prayer, a two-hour God-ordained phone conversation, and the divine leading of Holy Spirit to meet Debra face-to-face, we made the decision to retain Debra's services in order to seek the will and justice of our heavenly Father for Zack's life through simple obedience and leaving all the consequences in His all-loving hands. Below is the follow-up to our phone conversation, back in early February:

> *"Hello, Debra –*
> *It was really wonderful visiting with you yesterday and when Zack called me last night he went on and on how grateful he was for what God is doing. I explained to him that every time I see an empty seat, whether it's in my office, a business meeting, a ministry function I take part in or a small group, discipleship class or in the midst of church fellowship, I always choose to believe and imagine him there with me in both the physical and spiritual, occupying that space and, or empty seat in 2017. These are things hoped for.*
> *I explained to Zack what you said, that no one thus far has ever received a sentence reduction or release through the new commutation laws of Oklahoma for a violent offence. But I am believing that God will allow Zack to be the first, because of how the scales of justice were stacked against him in that ever-so-popular Tomahawk County Jail in Nada, OK. And I believe it because of how he has been shaped, molded and groomed for ministry. Zack told me he is good either way! He realizes that it's better for the inmates that he do his remaining years behind bars—he now does his time as free as free can be.*
> *He has a different thought. He is wondering why we don't seek a sentence reduction from 20 years to 15 violent. This would put him at time served and released*

*immediately. He said that Chaplain Fox, the leader of Kairos and the Offended (lady in Nada) are willing to go in front of the court to give a character witness.*

*Let's face it. Twenty years in today's world, for a small flame by lighting a paper towel on fire in a concrete cell, with steel bars and a flameproof mattress, is hardly endangering the lives of others. Stupid and senseless, yes; hardened criminal and violent offender, no way! Zack was addicted to drugs and was probably on crystal-meth or under the influence of some other drug when he committed this act of stupidity: crystal meth and drugs that were brought into the system through the people running this corrupt jail. Absolutely craziness.*

*I often wonder what sentence they gave the man who had the 9mm pistol stashed in his mattress, and what they gave the guard who brought it in for him. I know that the other two Oklahoma men who were caught on videotape coming out of that cell with Zack, didn't receive a 20 year charge. This is not justice. This is trumping up charges and using the law to make an example out of a young boy with a drug problem and poor attitude.*

*Regardless, commutation or reduction, I believe God will place the way onto your heart. You will know clearly through signs and wonders how God wants to use you as His willing and blessed vessel to bring the super-natural into the natural realm, so all can see a miracle take place. I explained to Zack, this is how miracles take place:*

*Choosing to believe and walk out of both the truth (what God says), and reality (what God sees), by faith (what is unseen, non-logical, non-rational, and incomprehensible in mind)—all in order to release Gods blessing that originates in the throne-room of Heaven and flows down like living water through earthen-vessels with surrendered hearts. The cooperation of mankind while under the divine influence of God —allowing us to live, naturally supernatural.*

*I am excited to see all that our glorious Savior, King Jesus, will accomplish through our simple obedience (harkening attentively) …*

*Many blessings sent your way, Debra. Be blessed as you go.*

*In-Christ,*

*Tony Murfin"*

Well, today is Good Friday of Easter Holy Week, 2016. I will be leaving for Pushing, Oklahoma, next Friday for my fourth special visitation with Zackery—God is so good. I can't begin to tell you all the joy that rests deep within a father's heart knowing all God has done, is doing, and will do in our lives and the lives of our children— He showed me that *change* always begins within. Without my March 13th, 2008 encounter with the Holy Spirit and the ex-*change* God desired to make within one man, there might never have been *change* manifested within Zackery and hundreds and even thousands of others inside and outside those walls. Thanks be to God for the power of prayer and the divine hope we have in Him to give us the exchanged life of Christ Jesus who died so that we all might have eternal life.

Zack and I will be meeting Debra to discuss and pray together about Zack's early release. I am so excited to see what God plans to do in all this. Honestly I have no idea what He will do, but I know with all my heart it will reap goodness and His very best for all involved.

I believe and trust that this will be Zackery's last visitation as an inmate in a maximum security prison. I prophesy and come into agreement with my Heavenly Father that there will be many hundreds of thousands of visitations *behind the glass* and bars of prisons around the world; where a father and son of *A Father-Saving Son* will set the captives free to be the beautiful new creations in Christ they were always created to be, but have never been exposed to the truth of how God sees them, loves them, and desires to change them through the *Divine Exchange*.

I don't know where you might find yourself in this God-story today. Maybe you're a father or a mother; maybe you're a son or a daughter, but wherever you find yourself you can know with complete confidence that you and all the ones you love most in this world all arrived as separated sons and daughters of an All-Knowing, All-Forgiving, All-Loving *Father-Saving Son* who wants you to come home!

Please, Come Home ...

*"The Spirit of the Lord God is upon me, because the Lord has anointed me to bring the good news to the poor; He has sent me to bind up the brokenhearted, to proclaim liberty to the captives, and the opening of the prison to those who are bound; to proclaim the year of the Lords favor, and the day of vengeance of our God; to comfort all who mourn; to grant to those who mourn in Zion—to give them beauty for ashes, the oil of joy for mourning, the garment of praise for the spirit of heaviness; that they may be called oaks of righteousness, the planting of the Lord, that He may be glorified."*
*—Isaiah 61:1-3 (ESV)*

# Epilogue

## A Warriors Guardian

"Last night an Angel came in my dream
washing fresh wounds by a heavenly stream.
I watched from a distance couldn't help to but stare,
who would harm and Angel? It didn't seem fair.
His wings were broken, battered, and bruised,
his sword was dull, shield shattered and used.
At the stream I looked the angel in the eye,
I saw his pain and thought he could die.
The angel looked defeated, wounded and sad,
I ask him to tell me about the battle he had.
I'm a guardian angel, this is what I do
and I do my best to keep harm from you!
See, you have an enemy who is after your life
and you are constantly putting me under the knife.
I went to my Master, asked the Lord above,
why you chose to reject Him and his great love.
He said, be patient the time will prevail,
so I continued to fight these demands from Hell.
My wings have been broken protecting you my friend,
yet you put me in danger time and time again.
That's why I look battered, wounded, and sad,
you're the hardest to protect I've ever had.

I won't give up on you no I won't let go,
I'm your guardian angel so this you now know.
It took me a moment to comprehend what he said,
I began to look back on the life that I've had.
The close calls, near misses, and brushes with death
the visions and memories nearly took my breath.
I dropped to my knees thanking God for my friend
and promised to never do those things again.
The angel assured me his wounds would all heal,
then I awoke and knew that my angel was real."
Zackery Murfin

# Notes

# Notes

# Notes

# Notes

# Notes

# Notes

# About the Author

Tony Murfin–CEO, Founder and Servant Leader of Ground Zero Electrostatics, an international static control company headquartered in Bradenton, Florida. Established in 1997, Ground Zero has been blessed to work with some of the largest Fortune 500 companies in the high-tech electronics world. Tony has been in marketplace ministry from the time he surrendered his life and the business back to its rightful Owner—Jesus Christ—back in 2008.

Since his radical life transformation and the divine exchange, Tony has had a heart surrendered to Jesus Christ for the advancement of the Kingdom and for the betterment of mankind. He has an unwavering passion and boldness to give Jesus away to all who enter his circle; that they may become one and alive with Christ.

As Tony travels the world on business and pleasure under the influence of Christ, he acts as the catalyst for others to experience the depths of our Creator's love, intimacy and oneness. Tony is extensively involved in world missions and has a heart for echoing the life, love and truth of Jesus as he goes, and everywhere he goes.

Tony and his amazing wife, Bimini, have been married and together for the past 28 years. Bimini is the willing vessel God used to pray Tony into the strong saving arms of Jesus his Lord. Tony and Bimini have been entrusted with three beautiful daughters, making the Tribe of Murfin six in total. Of course, their only begotten son is Zackery "Zack" Eugene (34); Karagan "KarBear" Marie (15); Kiah "Papaya" Kailey (14); Katalina "KitKat" Susan (3). The Murfin's reside in paradise alongside the white sandy beaches of Florida's westcoast.

Printed in the United States
By Bookmasters